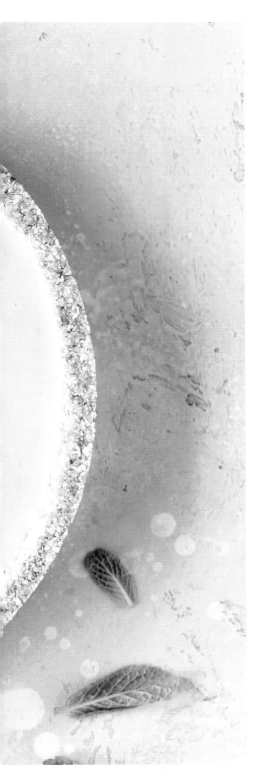

Cakes and Tarts

From comforting originals such as the Creamy Pistachio Tart (page 27) to remakes of traditional cakes such as the Black Forest Gateau (page 14) and Lemon Meringue Pie (page 31), in the following pages you'll find recipes to help you embrace every season and mood.

My Strawberry and Vanilla Panna Cotta Tart (page 17) or Mojito Tart (page 33) are perfect for both spring and summer; they are light, fruity and refreshing when enjoyed on those long warmer days. For those colder months, try out the Pumpkin Spice Latte Pie (page 28) or Apple and Custard Tart (page 18), which are packed with warm autumnal and wintry vibes.

The Black Forest Gateau (page 14) and I go way back even before I was born! My mother was nine months pregnant at the time and was hand delivering the cake to her neighbor (my late godfather) for his birthday. She slipped and fell belly-first into the gateau—the cake didn't make it, but I did. Many years later, I hope my vegan version of the cake does it justice!

Black Forest Gateau

Gluten-Free

This cake is possibly one of my favorites in the entire book, as it re-creates each layer used in the traditional cake using simple ingredients such as fruit and nuts. It's made up of decadent chocolate cake, sweet cherries and creamy coconut layers, which all complement one another perfectly.

MAKES ONE 6.5-INCH (16.5-CM) CAKE

CHOCOLATE CAKE

4 cups (468 g) walnuts

½ tsp Himalayan pink salt

½ cup (44 g) cacao powder

16 Medjool dates, pitted

1 tsp coconut oil (solid)

CHERRY SAUCE

3 cups (465 g) frozen cherries

⅓ cup (80 ml) maple syrup

¾ cup (180 ml) apple juice

2½ tbsp (20 g) cornstarch

CREAM

3 (13.5-oz [400-ml]) cans chilled coconut milk (using only the thick cream from the top of the can)

3 tbsp (45 ml) maple syrup

2½ tsp (13 ml) vanilla extract

3 oz (85 g) dark vegan-friendly chocolate, grated, for garnish

6 to 10 fresh cherries, for garnish

Note: Because of the fresh coconut cream in this cake, it's important to keep it chilled.

Start by making the cake base. Put the walnuts, salt and cacao powder into a food processor and blitz until they form a crumb consistency. Add the dates and coconut oil and blend until all the ingredients are combined and reach a dough consistency. Transfer the dough to a large bowl and knead it with your hands, then split the dough into three parts. Roll out each piece of dough between two sheets of parchment paper to about ½ inch (1.25 cm) thick. Use a 6.5-inch (16.5-cm) cake pan to cut the dough into three even circles. Carefully stack the dough bases on a plate between sheets of parchment paper and place in the freezer for 1 hour.

Meanwhile, prepare the cherry sauce. Put the cherries, maple syrup and apple juice in a saucepan and simmer for 20 minutes. Remove about 6 tablespoons (90 ml) of the cherry liquid and mix in a separate bowl with the cornstarch to form a paste. Add the cornstarch paste back to the saucepan and cook for 2 minutes, stirring continuously. Remove the sauce from the heat and set aside to cool for 15 minutes before refrigerating for 1 hour.

For the cream, put the thick coconut cream, maple syrup and vanilla in a large bowl and beat with an electric mixer until smooth and thick. Transfer half of the cream to a large piping bag fitted with an open star tip. Secure the top of the piping bag with an elastic band and place in the fridge to chill for 1 hour. The remaining cream can be stored in the fridge in an airtight container and used to decorate the cake later.

Once all of the ingredients are completely chilled, begin assembling the cake on a baking sheet or plate lined with parchment paper. Start with one cake base and add a layer of the cherry sauce. Pipe on a layer of the cream and top it with the next cake base. Repeat the process for the next layer until you finish with the third cake base. At this stage, it helps to place the layered cake into the freezer for 30 minutes or so to help the layers set.

Remove the cake from the freezer. If the edges are uneven, use a large bread knife to carefully trim them off. Place the remaining cream in a piping bag fitted with an open star tip. Pipe cream around the sides and top of the cake. Use a cake scraper or palette knife to smooth out the sides, top and edges of the cake. Decorate with more piped cream, grated chocolate and fresh cherries and serve.

This cake can be stored refrigerated in an airtight container for up to 2 days.

No-Bake

VEGAN DESSERTS

No-Bake

VEGAN DESSERTS

INCREDIBLY EASY PLANT-BASED CAKES, COOKIES, BROWNIES AND MORE

Christina Leopold

FOUNDER OF ADDICTED TO DATES

PAGE STREET
PUBLISHING CO.

Distributed by Macmillan, sales in Canada by The Canadian Manda Group.

24   23   22   21   20   1   2   3   4   5

ISBN-13: 978-1-64567-118-3
ISBN-10: 1-64567-118-6

Library of Congress Control Number: 2019957306

Cover and book design by Molly Gillespie for Page Street Publishing Co.
Photography by Christina Leopold
Author photographs by MRN Photography

Printed and bound in China

This book is dedicated to everyone who has helped in bringing this project to life, whether we know each other in person or have exchanged words online. This book is the result of the support and encouragement from you.

I hope the following pages can inspire you as much as you've inspired me to write them.

And to everyone who is out there, trying to make a difference in the world, thank you.

Contents

Introduction

WHY NO-BAKE?

Imagine being able to make delicious vegan desserts with minimal effort and maximum flavor.

A few years back, if you had told me that I could make brownies from just three ingredients that I already had in my pantry, I probably wouldn't have believed you! Especially not if those three ingredients were as simple as dates, nuts and cacao powder. No-bake is amazing because the recipes are incredibly easy to make. When baking is involved, there is a real science to it; precise measurements, timings and temperatures are key to the success or failure of a recipe.

I went vegan in 2015 after researching more about industries involving animal use and how animals are exploited for food, entertainment, clothing and research. I no longer wanted to contribute to those industries and realized that I would need to make some changes to my lifestyle in order to live in alignment with my morals. Even though it was just a few years ago, back then vegan-friendly products weren't as readily available here in rural Ireland as they are nowadays. I was intrigued by how easily no-bake recipes came together to create something delicious and instantly fell in love with them, which encouraged me to start creating recipes at home.

No-bake is great for me, as I love to be creative and adapt ingredients. I always feel like I have much more control of the end result of a dish throughout the entire "no-bake" process. The ability to change recipes and add a little more wet or dry ingredients during the recipe development stage gives no-bake recipes a great edge over baking. With baking, generally if you've made a mistake with ingredient ratios, it will only be discovered when you take the dish out of the oven. At this stage, it's almost guaranteed to be too late to make any adjustments that could potentially save the dish.

The no-bake recipes in this book are quite nutritionally dense. With lots of whole-food ingredients such as dates, nuts, fruits and seeds taking center stage in most of the recipes, the end products are filling and satiating. Don't get me wrong, they're still desserts, but with most of the recipes being free of refined sugar, they are a way to treat yourself, just a little better! The vast majority of the recipes are sweetened with dates, maple syrup or coconut sugar. Some of the recipes call for vegan chocolate as an ingredient. If you're avoiding overly processed white sugar, I recommend making my Mylk Chocolate recipe on page 124, which is sweetened with coconut sugar. Be sure to check the labels of plant-based milks and yogurts, and opt for sugar-free varieties. A lot of the ingredients used are raw and minimally processed, making them a healthier alternative to conventional sweets and desserts—a win-win!

With this book, my aim is to give you the tools you need to get started on your creative journey into the plant-based world of desserts. Whether you're someone who's a long-term vegan looking to get your creative juices flowing in the kitchen and inspire those around you to eat a plant-based diet, someone who's vegan-curious and looking to learn more about plant-based alternatives or someone looking for recipes to suit their specific dietary requirements, these simple and delicious desserts will satisfy the taste buds of even your most skeptical meat-eating relatives. The best stories come from people who have tried and shared my recipes with their non-vegan family, friends and work colleagues, opening up positive conversations and common ground surrounding plant-based eating and veganism.

Through developing recipes, I have found that food is an incredible way to bring people together. A few years ago on Instagram, I started to post pictures of my plant-based breakfasts hoping it could be of some inspiration to someone. I didn't know at the time that it would grow into an incredible community that I could connect with through food and still do to this day. There is nothing more rewarding to me than when someone enjoys something I've created or tries one of my recipes out themselves. Sharing pictures and recipes with an interesting audience from all over the world, and sharing tips, ideas, values and words of encouragement has been such an invaluable factor in being able to sit here and write this book today. From those Friday nights and weekends spent cramming in as many recipes as my freezer could hold before arriving back in the office on a Monday morning to now being able to focus fully on doing what I love, it's been an incredible journey on which I'm excited to continue.

I feel incredibly privileged to now be able to manifest these recipes into something physical, bringing the pictures from your screen to the pages of this book.

Christina Leopold

Strawberry and Vanilla Panna Cotta Tart

No-bake cakes tend to be rich and heavy. Using coconut milk along with a gelling agent gives desserts a light end result. With a light and creamy filling and fruity strawberry jam, this one's perfect for summer! Although you can use store-bought strawberry jam, I recommend taking this recipe to the next level with my Strawberry and Vanilla Bean Jam found on page 152.

MAKES ONE 9-INCH (23-CM) TART

CRUST

1¼ cups (182 g) cashews

1½ cups (150 g) rolled oats
(use gluten-free if required)

½ tsp sea salt or Himalayan
pink salt

2 tbsp (30 ml) maple syrup

3 tbsp (45 ml) creamed coconut
or coconut butter

Strawberry and Vanilla Bean Jam
(page 152) or store-bought

FILLING

1 vanilla pod

1 full (13.5-oz [400-ml]) can
coconut milk, plus 1 (13.5-oz
[400-ml]) can chilled coconut milk
(using only the thick cream from
the top of the can)

½ tsp vanilla extract

½ cup (120 ml) maple syrup

2 tbsp (16 g) cornstarch

1 tsp agar-agar (see Note)

1 cup (144 g) fresh strawberries
(cut into halves), for garnish

Note: Agar-agar is a plant-based gelatin obtained from red algae. This is a flavorless yet powerful setting agent for tarts, jelly and desserts.

To make the crust, put the cashews, oats and salt in your food processor and blitz for a couple of minutes until the ingredients form a light crumb consistency. Add the maple syrup and creamed coconut and blitz again until the mixture sticks together when you press it between your fingers.

Take a 9 x 3–inch (23 x 7.5–cm) cake pan with a removable bottom and line the bottom with parchment paper. Using a rubber spatula, press the dough into the bottom and sides of the pan (working approximately 2 inches [5 cm] up the edges). Ensure that the dough is firmly packed by pressing down on it with the flat bottom of a glass.

Spoon some of the strawberry jam onto the base of the tart in an even layer, about ¼ inch (6.5 mm) thick, and place in the freezer while you prepare the rest of the tart.

To prepare the filling, cut the vanilla pod in half lengthways and scrape out the seeds with a knife. Put the scraped vanilla pod and seeds in a saucepan with the coconut milk and bring to a simmer. (Reserve the remaining half of the pod for another use.) Add the vanilla extract and maple syrup and whisk well.

In a small bowl, mix the cornstarch and agar-agar. Pour approximately ½ cup (120 ml) of the warmed coconut milk mixture into the bowl and whisk well to form a paste. Add the cornstarch paste back to the pan with the remaining coconut milk and bring to a boil over high heat. Allow to simmer for 2 minutes, lowering the heat back to medium, while continuously whisking. Then strain the mixture through a fine-mesh sieve into a clean bowl.

Pour the mixture into the cake base and allow it to cool slightly for about 5 minutes before placing it in the fridge to set for at least 4 hours. Once set, carefully remove the tart from the pan, using a sharp knife to loosen around the edges and make sure the crust isn't sticking to them.

Garnish with fresh strawberries and serve.

Store the cake in an airtight container in the fridge for up to 5 days or alternatively freeze and defrost as needed before serving.

Apple and Custard Tart

There is something comforting about the combination of tart apples, creamy custard and spicy cinnamon. This no-bake version is made much healthier than the refined sugar— and dairy-laden version I used to have growing up. It's made up of an oat-y crust, filled with a light custard and topped with crisp, tart apples that don't lose their crisp texture or discolor.

MAKES ONE 8-INCH (20.5-CM) TART

CRUST

½ cup (84 g) roasted buckwheat or raw buckwheat toasted according to instructions (see page 21)

1 cup (100 g) rolled oats (use gluten-free if required)

¼ cup (48 g) coconut sugar, plus more for garnish

1 tsp ground cinnamon

½ tsp Himalayan pink salt

3 tbsp (47 g) almond butter

1½ tbsp (21 g) coconut oil (solid)

APPLE TOPPING

Juice of 2 lemons

½ cup (120 ml) water

2 tbsp (16 g) caster sugar

4 Gala or Pink Lady apples

CUSTARD FILLING

2 cups (480 ml) vanilla soy milk (substitute with regular soy, oat or coconut milk)

¼ cup (60 ml) maple syrup

1 vanilla pod

1 tsp agar-agar

1 tbsp (8 g) ground arrowroot

To make the crust, put the roasted buckwheat, rolled oats, coconut sugar, cinnamon and salt in your food processor and blitz to a fine crumb. Add in the almond butter and coconut oil and blend further until the mixture begins to stick together to form a dough consistency.

Take an 8-inch (20.5-cm) tart tin with a removable bottom and line the bottom with parchment paper. Transfer the crust mixture into the tart tin and press it down firmly into the bottom and sides of the dish using a rubber spatula or the flat bottom of a glass. Once the base is even and compact, put it in the freezer to set while you prepare the filling.

To prepare the apple topping, put the lemon juice, water and sugar into a saucepan. Bring to a simmer over medium heat and stir until all of the sugar has dissolved. Remove the saucepan from the heat and transfer the liquid to a bowl.

Core and slice the apples thinly, using a mandoline if possible, so that they are even. Once cut, immediately toss the apples in the lemon syrup to prevent discoloration. Make sure the apple slices are evenly coated with the juice and allow them to soak for 5 minutes. Then sit them on a clean towel or kitchen roll to remove any excess moisture.

For the custard filling, put the vanilla soy milk and maple syrup in a saucepan and bring to a simmer. Scrape out the seeds from the vanilla pod and add them to the pan along with the vanilla pod itself.

In a separate bowl, mix the agar-agar and arrowroot with 4 table-spoons (60 ml) of the custard liquid. Whisk well to form a paste and add to the saucepan once the rest of the mixture is simmering. Continue to whisk and cook the mixture for 5 minutes before passing it through a fine-mesh sieve to remove the vanilla pod.

Pour the custard mixture into the tart base and immediately start adding rows of sliced apples to garnish the cake. Once you have decorated the tart, transfer it to the fridge to set for about 4 hours.

Sprinkle with some coconut sugar before serving. Store in the fridge in an airtight container for up to 3 days.

Banoffee Pie

This no-bake version of traditional banoffee pie tastes just as good as the real thing and is sure to hit the spot for any banoffee lovers out there. The layers include an oat-y base, a creamy filling and sticky date caramel topped with fresh banana, coconut cream, caramel sauce and chocolate shards. This combination not only makes this pie irresistible but also super-easy to make, as it doesn't even require you to turn on the oven!

MAKES ONE 9-INCH (23-CM) PIE

CRUST

1 cup (168 g) roasted buckwheat or raw buckwheat toasted according to instructions provided

2 cups (200 g) rolled oats (use gluten-free if required)

½ tsp pink Himalayan salt

4 tbsp (56 g) coconut oil (solid)

3 tbsp (45 ml) maple syrup

¼ tsp ground nutmeg

FILLING

1½ cups (219 g) cashews (dry weight)

2 large ripe bananas

1 cup (240 ml) vanilla soy milk (or regular soy milk)

1 tsp vanilla extract

1 tbsp (14 g) coconut oil (solid)

½ tsp ground cinnamon

2 tbsp (30 ml) maple syrup

CARAMEL

9 Medjool dates, pitted

½ cup (129 g) peanut butter

½ cup plus 3 tbsp (165 ml) maple syrup

1 tsp pink Himalayan salt

Ahead of time, begin by preparing the cashews for the filling. Soak the cashews in water for a minimum of 4 hours before rinsing with clean water and draining them, or quick soak in boiled water for 1 hour.

If you are using raw buckwheat groats, you will need to toast them. Using a pan over medium heat, roast them in batches for 4 to 5 minutes until they begin to brown, tossing them so they brown evenly. Allow them to cool before using.

To prepare the crust, put the buckwheat, oats and salt in your food processor and blitz until they form a tight crumb consistency. Add in the coconut oil, maple syrup and nutmeg and blend until the mixture begins to stick together to form a dough.

Line the bottom of a 9 x 3–inch (23 x 7.5–cm) cake pan with some parchment paper before pressing the dough into the bottom and approximately 2½ inches (6.5 cm) up the sides of the pan. Use the flat bottom of a glass to smooth out the dough evenly. Trim the top edges with a knife to make them smooth and even. Set aside in the freezer while you make the rest of the pie.

For the filling, put all the filling ingredients in your high-speed blender and blitz until smooth and creamy without any lumps. Pour the mixture into the pan and tap the tin on your counter to knock out any air bubbles. Place in the freezer to set for 2 hours.

Clean your blender and next make the caramel by putting all of the ingredients in it and blitzing them until they form a smooth paste. Remove the pie from the freezer, spoon the caramel on top of the pie and smooth out using a spatula. Place the pie back in the freezer to set fully for another 2 hours.

(continued)

Banoffee Pie (continued)

TOPPING

2 large bananas

Juice of ½ lemon or 1 lime

COCONUT CREAM

1 (13.5-oz [400-ml]) can chilled coconut milk (using only the thick cream from the top of the can)

½ tsp vanilla extract

1 tsp maple syrup

SAUCE

2 tbsp (32 g) peanut butter

4 tbsp (60 ml) maple syrup

Dark chocolate chunks, for garnish (optional)

Once ready, remove the pie from the pan while still frozen. Slice the bananas into coins and dip them into the lemon juice. This will prevent them from discoloring. Put them on a sheet of parchment paper to remove any excess moisture. Arrange the banana coins in a circular design to cover the entire top of the tart.

For the cream, put the coconut milk, vanilla extract and maple syrup in a bowl and whisk using your electric mixer until soft peaks form. Transfer the cream to a piping bag fitted with an open star tip and pipe some peaks on top of the pie.

Lastly, to prepare the sauce, put the peanut butter and maple syrup in a bowl and whisk until smooth. Drizzle the sauce on top of the pie, sprinkle with dark chocolate chunks, if desired, and serve.

This pie will store for a few days refrigerated in an airtight container, or alternatively freeze and defrost as needed.

Dark Chocolate-Earl Grey Tart with Blackberry Coulis *Gluten-Free*

This decadent dark chocolate tart is incredibly simple to make. I love infusing recipes with tea, as it adds another dimension of flavor and sophistication to the dessert. The floral notes of Earl Grey black tea perfectly complement the dark chocolate, and the tart blackberry coulis offsets the sweetness of the chocolate for a balanced flavor experience.

MAKES ONE 9-INCH (23-CM) TART

CRUST

⅓ cup (54 g) roasted buckwheat or raw buckwheat toasted according to instructions (see page 21)

1 cup (146 g) cashews

⅔ cup (78 g) walnuts

¼ tsp Himalayan pink salt

3 Medjool dates, pitted

1 tbsp (14 g) coconut oil (solid)

1 tbsp (14 ml) maple syrup

3 tbsp (16 g) cacao powder

FILLING

2 (13.5-oz [400-ml]) cans chilled coconut milk (using only the thick cream from the top of the can)

6 Earl Grey tea bags

⅓ cup (80 ml) maple syrup

1 tsp vanilla extract

¼ tsp Himalayan pink salt or sea salt

3.75 oz (106 g) good-quality dark chocolate (dairy-free)

For the crust, put the buckwheat in your food processor and blitz for a couple of minutes, until roughly ground. Add the cashews, walnuts and salt and blitz for another minute or so, until the texture resembles a light crumb consistency. Add the dates, coconut oil, maple syrup and cacao powder and continue to process until all the ingredients start to stick together to form a dough.

Line the bottom of a 9-inch (23-cm) springform cake pan with parchment paper. Press the dough evenly into the bottom using a rubber spatula or the flat bottom of a glass, bringing the base approximately 2 inches (5 cm) up the sides to create a crust. Set the base aside in the freezer while you make the filling.

To make the filling, put the coconut milk and Earl Grey tea bags in a saucepan and bring to a boil over medium heat. Allow to simmer for about 5 minutes before carefully removing the tea bags. Add the maple syrup, vanilla extract and salt to the pan and whisk well.

Remove the saucepan from the heat and add the chocolate to the mixture. Allow it to melt through before whisking well to ensure the mixture is smooth and without lumps.

Remove the base from the freezer and pour the filling into it. Tap the pan on your work surface a couple of times to knock out any air bubbles.

(continued)

BLACKBERRY COULIS

1½ cups (216 g) frozen blackberries

3 tbsp (36 g) coconut sugar

½ cup (120 ml) orange or apple juice

1 cup (144 g) fresh blackberries, for garnish

Fresh mint leaves, for garnish

Allow the tart to cool for 10 to 25 minutes before placing it in the fridge to set for 4 hours. Once set, gently cut around the inside edges with a knife before removing the tart from the pan.

For the blackberry coulis, place the blackberries, coconut sugar and orange or apple juice into a heavy-bottomed saucepan. Place a lid on the saucepan and bring the mixture to a boil over high heat. Remove the lid, reduce the heat and allow the mixture to simmer for 10 to 20 minutes, until it has reduced by half.

Strain the mixture through a fine-mesh sieve and allow the liquid to cool, about 20 minutes, and set to a syrup consistency.

Decorate the tart with fresh blackberries and mint leaves and serve with a drizzle of blackberry coulis.

This tart will store for a few days refrigerated in an airtight container, or alternatively freeze and defrost as needed.

Creamy Pistachio Tart

This creamy tart has become one of my signature dishes. The light notes of vanilla and almond make the pistachio flavor sing in this recipe. It's creamy and light and melts in the mouth. A great alternative to cashew-based cheezecakes.

MAKES ONE 9-INCH (23-CM) TART

CRUST

1 cup (168 g) roasted buckwheat or raw buckwheat toasted according to instructions (see page 21)

1 cup (100 g) rolled oats (use gluten-free if required)

¼ tsp Himalayan pink salt

¼ cup (22 g) cacao powder

6 Medjool dates, pitted

3 tbsp (42 g) coconut oil (solid)

3 tbsp (45 ml) maple syrup

FILLING

1½ cups (185 g) shelled pistachios

1 (13.5-oz [400-ml]) can chilled coconut milk (using only the thick cream from the top of the can)

½ cup (120 ml) vanilla soy yogurt (or plain soy or coconut yogurt and ½ tsp vanilla bean paste)

½ cup (120 ml) maple syrup

4 tbsp (56 g) coconut oil (solid)

1 tsp almond extract

½ tsp wheatgrass or matcha powder (optional, for extra color)

TOPPING

¼ cup (31 g) chopped pistachios

2 oz (57 g) chopped dark chocolate

¼ cup (5 g) freeze-dried strawberries or raspberries, chopped

Dried roses

Ahead of time, begin by soaking the pistachios. Put them in a large bowl and cover with water for 4 hours. Rinse the pistachios with clean water and remove as much of the skin as possible. They should come off easily using your fingers, as the water will have loosened them.

To make the crust, put the buckwheat, oats, salt and cacao powder in your food processor and process to a light crumb consistency. Add the dates, coconut oil and maple syrup and continue to process until the ingredients begin to stick together and form a dough-like consistency.

Line the bottom of a 9-inch (23-cm) springform cake pan with parchment paper. Press the dough into the bottom and approximately 2 inches (5 cm) up the sides to form a crust. You can use a rubber spatula or the flat bottom of a glass to smooth it out.

Trim the top edges of the crust with a knife to make them smooth and even. Set the base aside in the freezer while you prepare the filling.

To make the filling, put all the filling ingredients in your high-speed blender and blitz until completely smooth and creamy without any lumps.

Pour the mixture into the crust and tap the pan on your work surface to knock out any air bubbles. Place the tart into the freezer to set for 6 hours or overnight.

Once set, carefully remove the tart from the pan while still frozen.

Decorate the tart by placing chopped pistachios, chopped dark chocolate, freeze-dried strawberries or raspberries and rose petals around the outer surface of the cake. Allow to defrost for 40 to 60 minutes before serving.

This tart can be stored in the fridge in an airtight container for up to 4 to 5 days. Alternatively, freeze in sections and defrost as needed.

Pumpkin Spice Latte Pie

Pumpkin spice oat milk lattes are one of my favorite treats during autumn. The warm spices, sweet cream, pumpkin and espresso make such a comforting combination. This no-bake tart is incredibly easy to make and incorporates all the elements of a pumpkin spice latte with a sweet, coffee-infused base, creamy pumpkin latte filling and coconut cream topping.

MAKES ONE 8-INCH (20.5-CM) PIE

CRUST

1 cup (100 g) rolled oats (use gluten-free if required)

½ cup (73 g) cashews

¼ cup (48 g) coconut sugar

1 tbsp (10 g) instant coffee granules

⅛ tsp Himalayan pink salt

1 tsp pumpkin spice, homemade (page 121) or store-bought

2 tbsp (28 g) coconut oil (solid)

2 tbsp (31 g) almond butter

FILLING

½ cup (120 ml) pumpkin purée

1 (13.5-oz [400-ml]) can coconut milk

½ cup (120 ml) maple syrup

2 tsp (10 ml) vanilla extract

1 tbsp (8 g) cornstarch

¾ tsp agar-agar

CREAM TOPPING

1 (13.5-oz [400-ml]) can chilled coconut milk (using only the thick cream from the top of the can)

2 tbsp (30 ml) maple syrup

1 tsp vanilla extract

½ tsp almond extract

8 pecans, for garnish

Coconut sugar, for garnish

For the crust, put the oats, cashews, coconut sugar, coffee, salt and pumpkin spice in your food processor and blitz to a fine crumb consistency. Add the coconut oil and almond butter and continue to process until the mixture begins to stick together to form a dough.

Take an 8-inch (20.5-cm) tart tin with a removable bottom and line the bottom with parchment paper.

Transfer the crust mixture to the tin and press it down firmly into the bottom and sides using a rubber spatula or the flat bottom of a glass. Once the base is even and compact, place the tin into the freezer to set while you prepare the filling.

To make the filling, put the pumpkin purée, coconut milk, maple syrup and vanilla extract in a saucepan and bring to a simmer over medium heat. In a separate bowl, combine the cornstarch and agar-agar with 4 tablespoons (60 ml) of the heated pumpkin mixture and whisk to form a paste.

Add the cornstarch paste to the saucepan and simmer for 5 minutes while continuously whisking. Remove the saucepan from the heat and allow to cool for 5 to 10 minutes before pouring the mixture into the tart shell. Gently tap the tin on your work surface to knock out any air bubbles, then chill it in the fridge for at least 4 hours to set.

Meanwhile, prepare the coconut cream topping by beating the cream ingredients in a large bowl using an electric mixer. Cover the bowl and chill until you are ready to decorate the tart.

Once the tart has set, remove it from the tart shell. Transfer the coconut cream to a piping bag fitted with an open star tip and pipe on top of the tart. See image for piping design ideas.

Garnish with pecans and coconut sugar before serving.

Store in an airtight container in the fridge for up to 3 to 4 days or freeze and defrost as needed.

Lemon Meringue Pie   *Gluten-Free*

A zingy and fresh lemon filling with caramelized soft meringue peaks and a complementary coconut base. This plant-based meringue doesn't require any baking and can be browned using a blowtorch to give it an aesthetic "toasted" look. Using a plant-based protein source such as aquafaba for the meringue makes it safe to eat unbaked, unlike classic meringues, which use eggs and need to be cooked.

MAKES ONE 9-INCH (23-CM) PIE

CRUST

1 cup (168 g) roasted buckwheat or raw buckwheat toasted according to instructions (see page 21)

½ tsp Himalayan pink salt

1 cup (93 g) dried shredded coconut

6 Medjool dates, pitted

1 tbsp (15 ml) lemon juice

1 tbsp (15 ml) maple syrup

1 tbsp (14 g) coconut oil (solid)

Almond flour or coconut flour, for dusting

LEMON CURD FILLING

1 (13.5-oz [400-ml]) can coconut milk

Grated zest of 2 organic lemons

Juice of 2 organic lemons

½ tsp ground turmeric

½ cup (120 ml) maple syrup

1½ tsp (6 g) agar-agar

2 tbsp (16 g) cornstarch

To make the crust, put the buckwheat and salt in your food processor and blitz for a minute or so to break down most of the buckwheat groats. Add the dried coconut and blend for another minute. Lastly, add the dates, lemon juice, maple syrup and coconut oil and blend until the mixture forms a dough.

Line the bottom of a 9-inch (23-cm) springform cake pan with parchment paper and spread the crust mixture out evenly on top of it. Using a rubber spatula or the flat bottom of a glass, press it down firmly into the bottom and approximately 2 inches (5 cm) up the sides of the pan. You can dust the base with a little almond or coconut flour to prevent the dough from sticking to your glass/spatula. Place the crust into the freezer to set while you prepare the filling.

For the filling, put the coconut milk, lemon zest, lemon juice, turmeric and maple syrup in a saucepan and bring to a simmer over medium heat. Simmer for 5 minutes before passing the mixture through a fine-mesh sieve to remove the lemon zest. Separate ¼ cup (60 ml) of the liquid in a small bowl and whisk the agar-agar and cornstarch with it to form a paste. Put the remaining liquid back into the saucepan along with the paste and bring to a boil over medium-high heat. Allow the mixture to cook for about 5 minutes while continuously whisking.

Once the mixture has thickened, remove it from the heat and allow to cool for 5 minutes before transferring it into the pie shell. Gently tap the pan on your work surface to knock out any air bubbles, and allow to cool for 10 to 15 minutes before transferring the pie to the fridge to set for at least 4 hours.

(continued)

Lemon Meringue Pie (continued)

SOFT MERINGUE TOPPING

½ cup (120 ml) aquafaba (the liquid from canned chickpeas; chill the can overnight and strain) (see Note)

1 tsp cream of tartar

½ tsp vanilla extract

⅓ cup (80 ml) water

1¼ tsp (5 g) agar-agar

¾ cup (90 g) caster sugar

To prepare the meringue topping, put the aquafaba and cream of tartar in a large bowl and beat using an electric mixer for 8 minutes. Add the vanilla extract and beat for 2 more minutes. The mixture will stiffen and should form stiff peaks.

Put the water, agar-agar and caster sugar in a saucepan and boil for 4 minutes. Remove the syrup from the heat and slowly add it to the aquafaba while whisking. Once incorporated, quickly transfer the meringue mixture to a piping bag fitted with an open star tip and pipe peaks on top of the lemon pie to cover the entire surface.

Allow the meringue to set for 30 minutes or so before using a blowtorch to brown the tops of the meringue peaks.

This pie is best served fresh but can also be stored in an airtight container in your fridge for a couple of days.

Note: Aquafaba is the liquid in which chickpeas or white beans have been cooked. It mimics the properties of egg whites and can be used to make vegan-friendly meringues, ice creams, marshmallows, mousses and much more. Simply refrigerate a can of chickpeas (garbanzo beans) or other neutral-tasting beans (such as cannellini) overnight and strain to separate the liquid.

Mojito Tart

This one is a twist on a classic favorite: Key lime pie. The light filling tastes like a refreshing cocktail. It's not too sweet and is completed with flavors of zested lime, fresh mint and rum essence that make this tart a big edible virgin cocktail!

MAKES ONE 9-INCH (23-CM) TART

CRUST

1½ cups (150 g) rolled oats (use gluten-free if required)

½ cup (47 g) dried shredded coconut

Zest of 1 lime

¼ tsp Himalayan pink salt

1 tsp dark rum essence or dark rum

2 Medjool dates, pitted

2 tbsp (30 ml) maple syrup

2 tbsp (28 g) coconut oil (solid)

Almond flour or coconut flour, for dusting

FILLING

Zest of 4 limes

Juice of 3 limes

1 (13.5-oz [400-ml]) can full-fat coconut milk

½ cup (120 ml) maple syrup

½ tsp rum essence

1 tsp wheatgrass or matcha powder (optional, for color)

5 fresh mint leaves

1 tbsp (8 g) ground arrowroot

1 tsp agar-agar

To make the crust, put the oats, coconut, lime zest and salt in your food processor and blitz until it reaches a fine crumb consistency. Add in the rum essence, dates, maple syrup and coconut oil and process until everything is combined.

Line the bottom of a 9-inch (23-cm) springform cake pan with parchment paper and spread the mixture out evenly on top of it. Roughly flatten out the dough using the flat bottom of a glass and then dust the dough with a little almond or coconut flour to prevent it from sticking. Using the glass, continue to press down the dough firmly into the bottom of the pan and approximately 1½ to 2 inches (4 to 5 cm) up the sides of the pan. Place the crust in the freezer to set while you prepare the filling.

For the filling, put the lime zest, lime juice, coconut milk, maple syrup, rum essence and wheatgrass powder in a saucepan. Bring the ingredients to a simmer over medium heat. Add in the mint leaves and simmer for 3 minutes. Pass the liquid through a fine-mesh sieve to remove the mint leaves and lime zest before returning the liquid back to the heat.

Meanwhile, mix the arrowroot, agar-agar and about ¼ cup (60 ml) of the filling mixture in a separate bowl. Whisk until the ingredients form a paste and then add them to the saucepan with the remainder of the coconut mixture. Bring to a boil while whisking continuously. Reduce to a simmer and cook for 2 minutes, whisking to ensure the mixture doesn't burn on the bottom.

Pour the filling into the crust and gently tap the pan on your work surface to remove any air bubbles. Allow the tart to cool for 10 to 15 minutes before placing it in the fridge to set for at least 4 hours.

(continued)

Mojito Tart (continued)

CREAM TOPPING

1 cup (240 ml) full-fat chilled coconut milk (using only the thick part from the top of a 13.5-oz [400-ml] can)

1 tbsp (15 ml) maple syrup

½ tsp vanilla extract

Fresh lime, sliced, for garnish

Fresh mint, for garnish

Fresh kiwi, cut into triangles, for garnish

Coconut sugar, for garnish (optional)

Meanwhile, to make the cream topping, put the coconut milk, maple syrup and vanilla in a bowl and beat with an electric mixer for 3 to 5 minutes, until smooth and thick. Place the cream in the fridge for 1 hour to help it to set before transferring it to a piping bag fitted with an open star tip.

Once the tart has set, carefully remove it from the pan, using a knife to loosen around the crust if it seems to be sticking. Pipe the whipped cream on top of the tart and decorate with sliced fresh lime, fresh mint leaves and kiwi. Sprinkle with coconut sugar, if desired, before serving.

Store in an airtight container in the fridge for up to 2 to 3 days.

Classic Candy

They say a picture is worth a thousand words, but I feel a recipe is worth many more. Recipes create memories, and certain foods can bring us back to a particular time in our lives. Some of our earliest memories are relived through nostalgic throwbacks to different food and treats; that apple tart or chocolate bar we enjoyed as a child. Thinking back to all the treats and sweets that I myself used to love years ago, they all had one thing in common—they were definitely not vegan friendly!

Take a trip down memory lane with nostalgic remakes of classic favorites. Creating vegan versions of childhood favorites are some of the most rewarding recipes to me. All the treats and chocolate bars that we used to enjoy can be created in a way that doesn't harm any animals.

In the following pages, you'll find everything from nutty Snickerz Chocolate Bars (page 38) to Jaffa No-Bakes (page 46) and my copycat Ferrawro Truffles (page 45). Being no-bake means they are incredibly easy to make, and the clever use of plant-based ingredients means you can reach the right consistencies and textures without having to turn on the oven!

I typically add a little bit of salt to all of my recipes as, when used in very low amounts, it tends to enhance their sweetness and overall adds another layer or dimension of flavor. Throughout this book, you'll see me refer to fine Himalayan pink salt, which is my favorite type to use. Feel free to substitute with the salt of your choice, although you can add more or less according to your taste, as some tend to have a higher sodium level.

These recipes are made to be shared, so pass them around, take them to school, bring them to the office and show the world how us vegans can have our cake and eat it, too!

Snickerz Chocolate Bars *Gluten-Free*

The combination of sweet caramel, salty peanuts and creamy chocolate makes these bars one of my most popular recipes. I made them at a local VegFest demonstration and everyone loved them so much. Made using plant-based, mainly whole-food ingredients, these chocolate bars are the ultimate guilt-free and cruelty-free dessert.

MAKES 12 LARGE OR 24 MINIATURE BARS

BASE

2 cups (292 g) raw, unsalted peanuts

¼ tsp Himalayan pink salt

10 Medjool dates, pitted

CARAMEL FILLING

10 Medjool dates, pitted (see Note)

½ cup (120 ml) rice milk

1 cup (258 g) crunchy peanut butter, divided

½ tsp Himalayan pink salt

1 tsp vanilla extract

1 cup (146 g) roasted peanuts (use unsalted if preferred)

CHOCOLATE COATING

9 oz (255 g) vegan-friendly chocolate, such as homemade Mylk Chocolate with Cashews and Lucuma (page 124)

1 tsp coconut oil (solid)

To make the base of the bars, blend the peanuts in your food processor until they form a light crumb. Add in the salt and dates and blend further for a few minutes, until completely combined and the ingredients stick together to form a doughy consistency.

Line a 12 x 3½–inch (30.5 x 9–cm) baking dish or similar-sized container with parchment paper and press the mixture evenly into the bottom of the dish using a rubber spatula. Set aside in the fridge while you make the caramel filling.

For the caramel, put the dates, rice milk, ½ cup (129 g) peanut butter, salt and vanilla extract in a high-speed blender and blitz until completely smooth. Transfer the caramel to a bowl and add the remaining ½ cup (129 g) peanut butter, then stir well to combine. Using your spatula, spread the caramel on top of the base.

Add the roasted peanuts on top of the caramel in an even layer. Place in the freezer to set for at least 4 hours or overnight.

Once set, remove the slab from the dish and place it on a cutting board.

Run hot water on your knife to heat it, then cut the slab into 12 large or 24 miniature bars. Place the bars back in the freezer while you prepare the chocolate coating.

For the coating, melt the chocolate and coconut oil in a double boiler over simmering water.

Dip the bars into the chocolate and sit them on top of a cooling rack lined with parchment paper to set. You can dip them a second time for a thicker layer of chocolate!

Store the bars in an airtight container in the fridge for up to a week or enjoy straight from the freezer.

Note: Dates are nature's caramel. They are not only naturally sweet, but they also help by working as a binding agent for many dessert bases. I usually opt for Medjool dates because of their soft texture and rich caramel flavor. Feel free to experiment with different varieties, and if using dates with a firmer texture, you can soak them in warm water beforehand to help soften them up.

Twix Bars

Gluten-Free

Gooey soft caramel and biscuit encased in a chocolate shell. The no-bake biscuit base of these candy bars means there's no fussing with ovens, just prep each layer and let the freezer do the rest of the work for you! The silicone molds I use for this are 3⅛ x 1⅛ x 1⅛ inches (79 x 29 x 29 mm) for large bars or use a 12 x 4-inch (30.5 x 10.25-cm) loaf pan for small candy bars.

MAKES 8 LARGE OR 14 SMALL BARS

CHOCOLATE COATING

7 oz (198 g) vegan-friendly chocolate, such as homemade Mylk Chocolate with Cashews and Lucuma (page 124)

1 tsp coconut oil (solid)

BASE

¾ cup (126 g) roasted buckwheat or raw buckwheat toasted according to instructions (see page 21)

⅛ tsp Himalayan pink salt

¼ cup (24 g) ground almonds or almond flour

1 tbsp (15 ml) tahini

2 tsp (9 g) coconut oil (solid)

1 tbsp (15 ml) maple syrup

CARAMEL

¼ cup (60 ml) light tahini

¼ cup plus 3 tbsp (105 ml) maple syrup

½ tsp Himalayan pink salt

2 tbsp (18 g) maca powder (see Note)

1 tbsp (14 ml) coconut oil (melted)

Note: Maca powder is a root powder that gives a wonderful "caramel" flavor to desserts while adding vitamins and minerals, too.

You can use silicone molds or a 12 x 4-inch (30.5 x 10.25-cm) loaf pan lined with parchment paper. If using the silicone molds, melt and mix the chocolate and coconut oil in a double boiler over simmering water. Put a layer of melted chocolate in the bottom of eight silicone compartments. Put in the freezer to set for 10 minutes and save the remaining chocolate for later in the recipe. Skip this step if you are using a baking dish and not individual molds.

To make the base, put the buckwheat and salt in your food processor and pulse until they form a rough flour consistency. Add the ground almonds, tahini, coconut oil and maple syrup and blend for a couple of minutes, until the ingredients begin to stick together to form a dough. Evenly distribute the dough between eight silicone mold compartments or use a 12 x 4-inch (30.5 x 10.25-cm) baking dish lined with parchment paper. Put in the freezer while you prepare the next layer.

For the caramel, put the tahini, maple syrup, salt and maca powder in a bowl. Whisk well to combine, then add in the melted coconut oil and whisk again until smooth. Divide the caramel between the eight bars or add as a layer if using a dish. Smooth out the caramel using the back of a spoon before placing the bars back in the freezer to set overnight or for a minimum of 6 hours.

Melt the leftover chocolate in a double boiler over simmering water. Remove the bars from the molds and sit them on a cooling rack with some parchment paper underneath to catch any melted chocolate. If you are using a dish, remove the dessert from the loaf pan and cut into bars using a sharp knife.

Dip the bars into the chocolate and coat them evenly before putting them on some parchment paper to set for about 30 minutes. You can place them in the fridge to help them set faster.

Once set, store the bars in an airtight container in the fridge for up to 1 week or enjoy straight from the freezer.

Jammy Wagon Wheels

I used to love to eat the store-bought version of these treats as a child. The flavors of marshmallow and jam encased in a biscuit and coated in chocolate pair so well together. This version is made without any products that use animals, such as dairy and gelatin.

MAKES 10 MEDIUM COOKIES

RASPBERRY JAM

¾ cup (188 g) frozen raspberries, defrosted

2 tbsp (20 g) chia seeds

2 tbsp (30 ml) maple syrup

OAT COOKIES

2 cups (200 g) rolled oats (use gluten-free if required)

½ tsp pink Himalayan salt

15 Medjool dates, pitted

3 tbsp (47 g) almond butter

CREAM FILLING

1 cup (240 ml) chilled coconut milk (using only the thick cream from the top of a 13.5-oz [400-ml] can)

2 tbsp (30 ml) maple syrup

1 tsp vanilla bean paste

CHOCOLATE COATING

6 oz (170 g) vegan-friendly chocolate or homemade Mylk Chocolate with Cashews and Lucuma (page 124)

1 tbsp (14 g) coconut oil (solid)

For the jam, put the raspberries in a saucepan, heat over medium heat until they begin to break down and bring to a simmer. Add the chia seeds and maple syrup and cook for 5 minutes. Remove from the heat and allow to cool.

To make the cookie base, blitz the oats and salt in your food processor until they reach a floury consistency. Add the dates and blend until the mixture forms a crumb. Add in the almond butter and blend further for 30 seconds. Transfer the mixture to a large bowl and press the dough together to form a ball.

With a rolling pin, roll the mixture between two sheets of parchment paper to a scant ½ inch (1.25 cm) in thickness. Cut circles out of the dough using a 2½-inch (6.5-cm) cookie cutter and set aside on a sheet of parchment paper. Reshape the remaining mixture and repeat until you have used up all of the dough. You should have 20 cookies total. Place the cookies in the freezer while you prepare the cream filling.

For the cream filling, whisk together the coconut milk, maple syrup and vanilla bean paste. Set the cream mixture aside in the fridge for 1 hour, or until it is firm enough to hold its shape.

To assemble the wagon wheels, put a small spoonful of the coconut cream on top of half the oat cookies and press down with the back of the spoon to flatten. Add a teaspoon of the jam on top and then sandwich with a second oat cookie.

Set the sandwiched cookies aside in the freezer while you melt and mix the chocolate and coconut oil in a double boiler over simmering water.

Dip the wagon wheels into the chocolate and sit them on a tray lined with parchment paper. Place in the freezer to set for 10 to 15 minutes.

Store in an airtight container in the fridge for up to 5 days or freeze and defrost as needed.

Ferrawro Truffles   *Gluten-Free*

These candies were such a treat back in the day. My take on the classic version replaces the dairy and refined sugar with healthier, plant-based ingredients. The truffle filling is made with my Notella recipe (page 148), which works perfectly to imitate the creamy chocolate-hazelnut filling that melts in the mouth.

MAKES 12 TRUFFLES

FILLING

½ batch Notella (page 148)

12 whole skinless hazelnuts

COATING

3.75 oz (106 g) vegan-friendly chocolate (homemade Mylk Chocolate with Cashews and Lucuma on page 124)

1 cup (120 g) skinless hazelnuts

Prepare the Notella, which will make up the filling for the pralines.

Use an oval-shaped silicone mold pan with at least 12 compartments to assemble the chocolates. (The dimensions for mine are 11¾ x 6¾ x 1¼ inches [30 x 17.25 x 3.25 cm].) Spoon the Notella mixture into the compartments and fill to the top. Press 1 whole hazelnut into the center of each one. Place the truffles in the freezer to set for at least 2 hours, until completely solid.

For the coating, melt the chocolate in a double boiler over simmering water and set aside in a bowl.

Put the hazelnuts in your food processor and pulse to break them down into small chunks.

Once the truffles have set, remove them from the molds and set them on a sheet of parchment paper. Keep the melted chocolate in one bowl and the ground hazelnuts in another and begin assembling the truffles.

Dip each truffle into the chocolate to coat them and then toss them in the ground hazelnuts. It's best to prepare them one by one, as the chocolate sets very quickly once it touches the frozen truffle!

Allow the truffles to set in the freezer for a few minutes before serving.

Store in the fridge in an airtight container for up to 1 week.

Jaffa No-Bakes   *Gluten-Free*

Growing up, the original Jaffa Cakes were always a popular cookie to have here in Ireland. Luckily, they are easily re-created in this no-bake, vegan-friendly and gluten-free version. The jelly part is even tasty on its own—good news, as you can munch on the trimmings while assembling these cookies!

MAKES 10 COOKIES

ORANGE JELLY

1 tbsp (6 g) orange zest

1 cup (240 ml) orange juice

4 tbsp (60 ml) maple syrup

1¼ tsp (5 g) agar-agar

¼ cup (60 ml) water

BASE

1 cup (146 g) cashews

1⅓ cups (128 g) almond flour or ground almonds

¼ tsp Himalayan pink salt

1 tsp orange zest

1 tbsp (14 g) coconut oil (solid)

Extra coconut oil or olive oil, for greasing

COATING

3.75 oz (106 g) vegan-friendly dark chocolate

½ tsp coconut oil (solid)

For the jelly, put the orange zest, orange juice and maple syrup in a saucepan and bring to a simmer over medium heat. In a separate bowl, mix the agar-agar and water until it has dissolved.

Add the agar-agar mix to the saucepan and bring to a boil over high heat while continuously whisking. Simmer for 5 minutes over medium-low heat and then remove from the heat.

Line the bottom and sides of an 8 x 4–inch (20.5 x 10.25–cm) cake pan or similar-sized container with parchment paper. Pour the orange mixture into the bottom and allow it to cool and set for 30 minutes.

Meanwhile, make the base by putting the cashews, almond flour, salt and orange zest in a food processor. Blitz to a crumb consistency and then add in the coconut oil and blend further, until the mixture sticks together like a dough.

Use coconut or olive oil to grease a bun baking tray. Get parchment paper and cut it into long strips. Put two strips in a cross shape in the bottom of each bun case—these will act as little handles and make it easy to lift the finished cakes from the tray once they're ready!

Divide the dough equally among the bun tray compartments and press the mixture into the bottoms to form the cookie part of each cake.

Use a 2-inch (5-cm) cookie cutter to cut circles out of the orange jelly and place one of them on top of each cookie. Remove the cookies from the tray and place them on a cooling rack.

To make the coating, melt and mix the chocolate and coconut oil in a double boiler over simmering water and spoon the melted chocolate on top of each cake. Use a fork to press a crisscross design into the top of each cake.

Transfer them to the fridge to cool for 30 minutes before serving.

Store in the fridge in an airtight container for up to 3 to 4 days or freeze and defrost as needed.

Salted Vanilla Bean and Cashew Butter Fudge   *Gluten-Free*

This is probably the simplest recipe in this book, but it's also probably one of my favorites! This no-bake fudge is prepared in minutes with only a few ingredients, and can be stored in your freezer so that you always have a stash of sweets on hand! Try adding it to warm oatmeal for a sweet, gooey and melty treat.

MAKES 20 TO 25 FUDGE PIECES

1 cup (258 g) cashew butter

¾ cup (180 ml) maple syrup

3 tbsp (42 g) coconut oil (solid)

1 tsp vanilla bean paste

½ tsp sea salt or Himalayan pink salt

Coarse sea salt, for garnish

Put the cashew butter, maple syrup, coconut oil, vanilla bean paste and salt in your food processor and blend for a few minutes, until everything is combined and the mixture is smooth and creamy. Line a 6 x 8–inch (15.25 x 20.5–cm) baking tray, dish or tub with parchment paper and transfer the fudge into the tray using a rubber spatula. Gently tap the tray on your work surface to knock out any air bubbles.

Transfer the tray to the freezer to set for 3 hours.

Once firm, sprinkle the fudge with some coarse sea salt and remove it from the tray.

Cut the fudge into chunks and serve.

Store the fudge in the freezer in an airtight container. It will last for several weeks.

Cheezecakes

Time to let your creativity shine through! Here are some exciting flavor combinations with simple yet extravagant cheezecakes that are perfect for birthdays and special celebrations.

In this chapter, you'll find indulgent flavors of cheezecakes such as white chocolate and passion fruit (page 55) and peanut butter and jelly (page 58), as well as lighter cakes for fruit lovers, such as blueberry and lemon (page 61) and fruity mango (page 70).

These no-bake cheezecakes are made with a cashew base, which gives them a creamy texture as well as a slightly tangy flavor. The cashews are prepared by soaking them in water—this not only makes them easier on your blender, but it also gives them a creamier consistency. Simply soak your cashews in water and leave them to sit for 4 hours before rinsing them with clean water.

Top tip: If you're in a hurry, you can "quick soak" your cashews by covering them with boiling water and allowing them to sit for 1 hour before rinsing.

Cherry Bomb Cheezecake *Gluten-Free*

This cake is any cherry lover's dream. The almond base tastes like marzipan and perfectly complements the layers of fruity cheezecake and sweet cherry sauce. Although you can use fresh dark cherries and cherry juice for this recipe, I find that frozen sour cherries give a nicer color. Plus, you are left with the liquid cherry juice when you defrost the cherries, so you don't need to go out and buy the juice separately!

MAKES ONE 8-INCH (20.5-CM) CAKE

CRUST

1½ cups (144 g) ground almonds or almond flour

¼ tsp Himalayan pink salt

7 Medjool dates, pitted

1 tsp almond extract

CHERRY CHEEZECAKE FILLING

1¾ cups (255 g) cashews (dry weight)

2 cups (310 g) frozen cherries, defrosted, juice reserved

1 (13.5-oz [400-ml]) can chilled coconut milk (using only the thick cream from the top of the can)

½ cup (120 ml) maple syrup

2 tsp (10 ml) vanilla extract

1 tsp almond extract

¼ cup plus 1 tbsp (71 g) coconut oil (solid)

1 tbsp (15 g) cashew butter

Pinch of Himalayan pink salt

Ahead of time, begin by preparing the cashews for the cheezecake filling. Soak the cashews in water for a minimum of 4 hours before rinsing with clean water and draining them, or quick soak in boiled water for 1 hour.

At the same time, fully defrost the 4 cups (620 g) of cherries for both the filling and the topping. Allow them to sit in a fine-mesh sieve over a bowl while they warm up. Reserve the juice for the topping of the cake. Squeeze the cherries to remove any excess juice, since if there is too much liquid in your filling mixture, it may not set properly.

To make the crust, put the ground almonds and salt in your food processor and blitz for 1 minute, until it's a fine crumb consistency. Add the dates and almond extract and process for a couple more minutes, until the mixture starts to stick together and form a dough.

Line the bottom of an 8 x 4–inch (20.5 x 10.25–cm) cake pan with parchment paper and press the dough evenly into the bottom using a rubber spatula or the flat bottom of a glass. Once even, put the base in the freezer while you prepare the next layer.

For the cheezecake, put the cashews, 2 cups (310 g) of cherries (without the juice) and all the remaining cheezecake filling ingredients into your high-speed blender. Blend the mixture on high speed until it's completely smooth and creamy. Remove the cake base from the freezer and pour the cheezecake mixture onto it, tapping the pan gently on your work surface to knock out any air bubbles. Place in the freezer to set for 6 hours or overnight.

(continued)

Cherry Bomb Cheezecake (continued)

CHERRY TOPPING

½ cup (120 ml) cherry juice (left over from defrosting the cherries)

2 tbsp (30 ml) maple syrup

1 tbsp (8 g) cornstarch

2 cups (310 g) fresh or frozen cherries, defrosted and pitted

For the cherry topping, put the cherry juice and maple syrup in a saucepan and bring the mixture to a simmer over medium heat. Meanwhile, combine the cornstarch with 4 tablespoons (60 ml) of the heated cherry juice in a separate bowl and mix well.

Add the cornstarch mixture to the saucepan and bring the mixture to a boil, whisking continuously. Reduce the heat and simmer for 5 minutes, making sure you keep stirring to avoid the mixture from sticking to the bottom of the pan.

Remove the saucepan from the heat and stir in the remaining 2 cups (310 g) of pitted cherries. Allow the cherry mixture to cool for about 10 minutes. Remove the cake from the pan while still frozen to keep the cake from sticking to the pan. Spread the cherry sauce mixture on the top of the cheezecake.

Allow the cake to defrost for 45 minutes to 1 hour before serving.

Store in an airtight container in your fridge and consume within 1 to 2 days. Alternatively, freeze any unused cake and defrost before serving.

White Chocolate and Passion Fruit Cheezecake

Gluten-Free

This decadent white chocolate cheezecake is complemented by sweet, tropical passion fruit for a match made in heaven. The cacao butter gives this cake its "white chocolate" flavor. When selecting a brand of cacao butter, it's best to go with a good-quality, raw version, as this will be the main flavor for the cheezecake.

MAKES ONE 8-INCH (20.5-CM) CAKE

CRUST

1 cup (146 g) cashews

1 cup (96 g) almond flour or ground almonds

¼ tsp Himalayan pink salt

5 Medjool dates, pitted

½ tbsp (7 g) coconut oil (solid)

WHITE CHOCOLATE FILLING

1½ cups (219 g) cashews (dry weight)

½ cup plus 2 tbsp (150 ml) maple syrup

⅔ cup (144 g) cacao butter

1½ cups (360 ml) vanilla soy yogurt (or plain soy or coconut yogurt)

1 tsp vanilla bean paste

PASSION FRUIT JELLY

8 passion fruits

⅓ cup (80 ml) maple syrup

½ tsp agar-agar

2 tbsp (30 ml) water

Ahead of time, begin by preparing the cashews for the cheezecake filling. Soak the cashews in water for a minimum of 4 hours before rinsing with clean water and draining them, or quick soak in boiled water for 1 hour.

To make the crust, put the cashews, almond flour and salt in your food processor and blitz for 1 minute, until it's a fine crumb consistency. Add the dates and coconut oil and process for a couple more minutes, until the mixture starts to stick together and form a dough.

Line the bottom of an 8 x 4–inch (20.5 x 10.25–cm) cake pan with parchment paper and press the dough evenly into the bottom using a rubber spatula or the flat bottom of a glass. Once even, sit the base in the freezer while you prepare the next layer.

For the white chocolate filling, put all the ingredients for the filling into your high-speed blender, including the soaked cashews. Blend the mixture on high speed until it's completely smooth and creamy. Remove the cake base from the freezer and pour the cheezecake mixture onto it, tapping the pan gently on your work surface to knock out any air bubbles. Place in the freezer to set for 6 hours or overnight.

For the passion fruit jelly, slice the passion fruits in half and scoop out the filling. Squeeze the filling through a fine-mesh sieve to separate the juice from the seeds. Reserve the seeds and put the passion fruit juice and maple syrup in a saucepan. Bring the mixture to a simmer over medium heat. Meanwhile, combine the agar-agar with the water in a separate bowl and mix well.

(continued)

White Chocolate and Passion Fruit Cheezecake (continued)

Add the agar-agar mixture to the saucepan and bring the mixture to a boil, whisking continuously. Reduce the heat and simmer for 5 minutes, making sure you keep stirring to avoid the mixture from sticking to the bottom of the pan. Take approximately half of the passion fruit seeds and add them to the jelly mixture, and whisk well.

Remove the jelly mixture from the heat and allow to cool slightly for about 5 minutes before pouring it on top of the cheezecake. Put the cheezecake back in the freezer for another hour or so until completely set.

Remove the cake from the pan while still frozen to keep the cheezecake from sticking to the pan. Allow to defrost for 45 minutes to 1 hour before serving.

Store in an airtight container in your fridge for up to 3 to 4 days or freeze and defrost before serving.

Peanut Butter and Jelly Cheezecake

Layers of creamy peanut butter cheezecake and fruity raspberry jelly on top of a peanut butter cookie base make this cake a showstopper and the perfect party centerpiece. As this cake is made in layers, it has a few components, so I recommend preparing this cake the day before you want to serve it and taking it out of the freezer the following morning to decorate with the finishing touches.

MAKES ONE 8-INCH (20.5-CM) CAKE

CRUST

½ cup (84 g) roasted buckwheat or raw buckwheat toasted according to instructions (see page 21)

1½ cups (150 g) rolled oats (use gluten-free if required)

½ tsp Himalayan pink salt

1½ tbsp (21 g) coconut oil (solid)

¼ cup (65 g) peanut butter

3 tbsp (45 ml) maple syrup

3 tsp (15 ml) water

PEANUT BUTTER CHEEZECAKE FILLING

3 cups (438 g) cashews (dry weight), divided

1¼ cups (300 ml) maple syrup, divided

1½ cups (387 g) peanut butter, divided

1 tsp vanilla bean paste, divided

¼ cup (56 g) coconut oil (solid), divided

½ cup (120 ml) soy yogurt, divided

½ cup (120 ml) chilled coconut milk (using only the thick cream from the top of a 13.5-oz [400-ml] can), divided

2 tbsp (30 ml) lemon juice, divided

Pinch of salt

Ahead of time, begin by preparing the cashews for the cheezecake filling. Soak the cashews in water for a minimum of 4 hours before rinsing with clean water and draining them, or quick soak in boiled water for 1 hour.

To make the crust, put the buckwheat in your food processor and blitz for 1 minute until it's a fine crumb consistency. Add the oats and salt and process for another minute until it's a floury consistency. Lastly, add the coconut oil, peanut butter, maple syrup and water and process for a couple more minutes, until the mixture starts to stick together and form a dough. Separate 1 cup (150 g) of the base mixture and set aside for making bliss balls to decorate the cake.

Line the bottom of an 8-inch (20.5-cm) springform cake pan with parchment paper and press the dough evenly into the bottom using a rubber spatula or the flat bottom of a glass. Once even, put the base in the freezer while you prepare the next layer.

For the cheezecake filling, put half of the filling ingredients in your high-speed blender. Blend the mixture on high speed until it's completely smooth and creamy.

Remove the base from the freezer and pour the cheezecake mixture onto the base, tapping the pan gently on your work surface to knock out any air bubbles. Place in the freezer to set for 1 hour.

While the first layer of cheezecake is setting, you can prepare the bliss balls that will be used to decorate the cake. Take the remaining cup of the crust mixture and add 1 teaspoon of water before kneading it to form a dough. Separate the dough into eight parts and roll them into balls. Place them in an airtight container and refrigerate until you're ready to decorate the cake later.

(continued)

Peanut Butter and Jelly Cheezecake (continued)

RASPBERRY JELLY

3½ cups (875 g) frozen raspberries

¼ cup (60 ml) maple syrup

2 tsp (8 g) agar-agar

⅓ cup (80 ml) water

PEANUT BUTTER CREAM

½ cup (120 ml) chilled coconut milk (using only the thick cream from the top of a 13.5-oz [400-ml] can)

1 tbsp (16 g) peanut butter

1 tsp maple syrup

Pinch of salt

¼ cup (37 g) roasted peanuts, chopped, for garnish (use unsalted if preferred)

To make the jelly, put the raspberries in a saucepan over medium heat, cook until they begin to break down and bring them to a simmer. Cook for about 5 minutes, stirring regularly to avoid burning. Pass the raspberries through a fine-mesh sieve, squeezing out any juice with the back of a spoon. Discard the seeds and transfer the liquid back to the saucepan. Add the maple syrup to the pan, bring to a simmer over medium heat and allow to reduce for another 5 minutes.

Meanwhile, in a small bowl, mix the agar-agar with the water. Whisk well and allow to sit for 2 minutes. Then add it to the pan with the raspberry liquid. Bring the mixture to a boil and then simmer for 5 minutes, whisking continuously. Remove the pan from the heat and allow to cool for 5 minutes.

Remove the base from the freezer and pour the raspberry jelly mixture on top of the cheezecake, making sure it's evenly distributed with a spatula if needed. Let it cool for 5 minutes before transferring back to the freezer to set for 10 minutes.

To prepare the next cheezecake layer, add the remaining half of the filling ingredients to the blender and blitz until smooth and creamy. Remove the base from the freezer and pour the cheezecake mixture on top of it. Smooth out the surface of the cake with a knife or spatula before transferring back to the freezer to set for a minimum of 4 hours or overnight.

Meanwhile, make the peanut butter cream. Put the coconut milk, peanut butter, maple syrup and salt in a bowl and beat using an electric mixer until smooth. Transfer the cream to a piping bag fitted with an open star tip and refrigerate until the cake is set.

Once set, remove the cheezecake from the pan while still frozen. Pipe the cream onto the top of the cake in eight parts to create nests on which to rest each of the bliss balls.

Sprinkle the chopped peanuts on top of the remaining surface area of the cake and serve.

Store in an airtight container in the fridge for up to 2 days or freeze any leftover cake and defrost as needed.

Blueberry and Lemon Cheezecake *Gluten-Free*

If you're in the mood for a fruity, summery dessert, this cake is the one for you. Zesty fresh lemon and creamy sweet blueberry work in harmony with one another in this layered cheezecake. It's the perfect combination of sweet and sour.

MAKES ONE 9-INCH (23-CM) CAKE

CRUST

1 cup (168 g) roasted buckwheat or raw buckwheat toasted according to instructions (see page 21)

¾ cup (70 g) dried shredded coconut

¼ tsp Himalayan pink salt

8 Medjool dates, pitted

2½ tbsp (35 g) coconut oil (solid)

LEMON CHEEZECAKE FILLING

1½ cups (219 g) cashews (dry weight)

1 (13.5-oz [400-ml]) can chilled coconut milk (using only the thick cream from the top of the can)

½ cup (120 ml) maple syrup

Zest of 2 organic lemons

Juice of 2 organic lemons

¼ tsp ground turmeric

1 tbsp (14 g) coconut oil (solid)

Ahead of time, begin by preparing the combined 3 cups (438 g) of cashews for both the blueberry and lemon cheezecake fillings. Soak the cashews in water for a minimum of 4 hours before rinsing with clean water and draining them, or quick soak in boiled water for 1 hour. Divide the soaked cashews into two parts for the separate lemon and blueberry cheezecake layers.

To make the crust, put the roasted buckwheat, shredded coconut and salt in your food processor and blitz for 1 minute until reaching a fine crumb consistency. Add the dates and coconut oil and process for a couple more minutes, until the mixture starts to stick together and form a dough.

Line the bottom of a 9-inch (23-cm) springform pan with parchment paper and press the dough evenly into the bottom using a rubber spatula or the flat bottom of a glass. Once even, sit the crust in the freezer while you prepare the next layer.

For the lemon cheezecake layer, add half of the soaked cashews and all of the other lemon cheezecake ingredients to your high-speed blender. Blend the mixture on high speed until it's completely smooth and creamy. Remove the crust from the freezer and pour the lemon cheezecake mixture onto it, tapping the pan gently on your work surface to knock out any air bubbles. Place in the freezer to set for 1 hour. Clean the blender.

(continued)

Blueberry and Lemon Cheezecake (continued)

BLUEBERRY CHEEZECAKE FILLING

1½ cups (219 g) cashews (dry weight)

1 (13.5-oz [400-ml]) can chilled coconut milk (using only the thick cream from the top of the can)

¾ cup (180 ml) maple syrup

½ cup (74 g) wild blueberries (defrosted if using frozen)

¼ cup (60 ml) vanilla soy milk

2½ tbsp (35 g) coconut oil (solid)

1 tsp vanilla bean paste

¼ tsp ground cinnamon

1 cup (148 g) fresh blueberries, for garnish

For the blueberry cheezecake layer, put the remaining half of the soaked cashews and all of the other blueberry cheezecake ingredients in the blender. Blend for a few minutes until smooth and creamy. Pour on top of the lemon layer, tap to knock out any air bubbles and place back in the freezer to set for 6 hours or overnight.

Allow the cake to defrost for 45 minutes to 1 hour and decorate with fresh blueberries before serving.

Store in an airtight container in your fridge for up to 3 to 4 days. Alternatively, freeze and defrost before serving.

Cookie Dough Cheezecake *Gluten-Free*

No-bake cookie dough is one of my favorite things. If you love cookie dough, then this recipe is perfect for you! A creamy vanilla cheezecake on a no-bake chocolate chip cookie dough base. Cookie dough balls are also placed inside the cheezecake to be revealed as you slice into the cake.

MAKES ONE 8-INCH (20.5-CM) CAKE

COOKIE DOUGH CRUST/BALLS

2¾ cups (264 g) almond flour or ground almonds

2½ tbsp (30 g) coconut sugar

½ tsp Himalayan pink salt

½ tsp ground cinnamon

2 tsp (10 g) cashew butter

¼ cup (60 ml) vanilla soy milk (or alternative plant milk mixed with 1 tsp vanilla extract)

½ cup (84 g) vegan-friendly chocolate chips

Ahead of time, begin by preparing the cashews for the cheezecake filling. Soak the cashews in water for a minimum of 4 hours before rinsing with clean water and draining them, or quick soak in boiled water for 1 hour.

For the crust, in a large bowl, mix the almond flour, coconut sugar, salt and cinnamon. In a separate bowl, whisk together the cashew butter and soy milk until smooth.

Next, add the wet ingredients to the dry ingredients and mix everything together using a rubber spatula or clean hands. Lastly, add in the chocolate chips and mix them in evenly.

Line the bottom of an 8-inch (20.5-cm) springform pan with parchment paper and add two-thirds of the cookie dough mixture, reserving the other third for cookie dough balls. Press the mixture down into the bottom of the pan using the flat bottom of a glass. Set it aside in the freezer while you prepare the rest of the cake.

Roll the remainder of the cookie dough into balls; it should make 12 or 13 small balls. Cover the balls and set them aside in the fridge for now.

(continued)

Cookie Dough Cheezecake (continued)

FILLING

1½ cups (219 g) cashews (dry weight)

1 (13.5-oz [400-ml]) can chilled coconut milk (using only the thick cream from the top of the can)

¾ cup (180 ml) vanilla soy yogurt

¼ cup (60 ml) maple syrup

Juice of ½ lemon

1 tsp vanilla bean paste

3 tbsp (45 ml) creamed coconut or coconut butter

½ tsp ground cinnamon

2.5 oz (71 g) vegan-friendly chocolate

1 tsp coconut oil (solid)

A few vegan-friendly chocolate chips, for garnish

For the filling, put all of the filling ingredients in your high-speed blender and blend on full speed for about 5 minutes, or until smooth and creamy and without any lumps. Pour half of the mixture into the pan, then add four of the cookie dough balls, pressing them down into the filling. Add the remainder of the filling followed by another four cookie dough balls, placing them evenly throughout the cake. Gently tap the pan on your work surface to knock out any air bubbles.

Transfer the cake to the freezer to set for at least 6 hours or overnight. Once the cake has set, remove it from the pan while still frozen to ensure it doesn't start to stick to the edges.

Melt and mix the chocolate and coconut oil together in a double boiler over simmering water and stir well. Using a spoon, drizzle the chocolate around the edges of the cake. Take your time with this to get it as precise and neat as possible.

Dip the rest of the cookie dough balls in some of the leftover melted chocolate and stick them to the top of the cake for garnish. Sprinkle the cake with some chocolate chips and serve.

Store in the fridge in an airtight container for up to 3 to 4 days or freeze and defrost before serving.

Turkish Delight Cheezecake

A cacao and rose cookie base topped with layers of strawberry and vanilla yogurt cheezecake topped with a strawberry-rose jelly. This cake has several layers; however, feel free to keep it to just one strawberry layer and one vanilla layer if you want to keep things simple or want to save some time!

MAKES ONE 9-INCH (23-CM) CAKE

CRUST

1½ cups (150 g) rolled oats (use gluten-free if required)

½ cup (73 g) cashews

¼ cup (22 g) cacao powder

¼ cup (48 g) coconut sugar

¼ tsp Himalayan pink salt

1 tbsp (15 ml) culinary rose water

3 tbsp (42 g) coconut oil (solid)

VANILLA CHEEZECAKE

1½ cups (219 g) cashews (dry weight)

1 (13.5-oz [400-ml]) can chilled coconut milk (using only the thick cream from the top of the can)

½ cup (120 ml) maple syrup

½ cup (120 ml) vanilla soy yogurt

½ tsp vanilla bean paste

2 tbsp (28 g) coconut oil (solid)

1 tbsp (15 ml) lemon juice

STRAWBERRY CHEEZECAKE

1½ cups (219 g) cashews (dry weight)

1 (13.5-oz [400-ml]) can chilled coconut milk (using only the thick cream from the top of the can)

½ cup (120 ml) maple syrup

½ cup (120 ml) soy yogurt

2 tbsp (28 g) coconut oil (solid)

¼ cup (36 g) fresh strawberries

1 cup (20 g) freeze-dried strawberries (or an additional ½ cup [72 g] fresh strawberries)

Ahead of time, begin by preparing the combined 3 cups (438 g) of cashews for both the vanilla and strawberry cheezecake fillings. Soak the cashews in water for a minimum of 4 hours before rinsing with clean water and draining them, or quick soak in boiled water for 1 hour. Divide the soaked cashews into two separate parts for the vanilla and strawberry cheezecake layers.

To make the crust, put the rolled oats, unsoaked cashews, cacao powder, coconut sugar and salt in your food processor and blitz for 1 minute, until it's a fine crumb consistency. Add the rose water and coconut oil and process for a couple more minutes, until the mixture starts to stick together and form a dough.

Line the bottom of a 9-inch (23-cm) springform cake pan with parchment paper and press the dough evenly into the bottom using a rubber spatula or the flat bottom of a glass. Once even, put the crust in the freezer while you prepare the next layer.

For the vanilla cheezecake, put all the vanilla cheezecake ingredients in your high-speed blender. Blend the mixture on high speed until it's completely smooth and creamy. Split the mixture in half, reserving one half for later. Remove the crust from the freezer and pour half of the cheezecake mixture onto it, tapping the pan gently on your work surface to knock out any air bubbles. Place in the freezer to set for 1 hour.

For the strawberry cheezecake, put all the strawberry cheezecake ingredients in the blender. Blend for a few minutes until smooth and creamy, then split the mixture in half, reserving one half for later. Pour one half on top of the vanilla layer, tap to knock out any air bubbles and place back in the freezer to set for at least 30 minutes.

Once the strawberry layer is slightly firm, pour the remaining half of the vanilla cheezecake mixture on top of it and tap out any air bubbles. Freeze for another 30 minutes to set and top with the remaining strawberry filling mix. Freeze the cake for at least another hour before preparing the jelly layer.

(continued)

Turkish Delight Cheezecake (continued)

STRAWBERRY-ROSE JELLY

1 cup (144 g) strawberries

⅓ cup (80 ml) maple syrup

¼ cup (60 ml) culinary rose water

¾ tsp agar-agar

1 scant cup (240 ml) water

Fresh strawberries, cut in half, for garnish

Freeze-dried strawberries, for garnish

Dried or fresh roses, for garnish

For the jelly, blend the strawberries, maple syrup and rose water and then press the mixture through a fine-mesh sieve into a saucepan over medium heat. Bring the mixture to a simmer. Meanwhile, combine the agar-agar with the water in a separate bowl and mix well.

Add the agar-agar mixture to the saucepan and bring the mixture to a boil, whisking continuously. Reduce the heat and simmer for 5 minutes, making sure you keep stirring to avoid the mixture from sticking to the bottom of the pan.

Remove the jelly mixture from the heat and allow it to cool for about 10 minutes before pouring it on top of the cheezecake. Put the cheezecake back in the freezer for another 4 hours or until completely set.

Remove the cake from the pan while still frozen to keep the cheezecake from sticking to the pan and allow to defrost for 45 minutes to 1 hour before serving.

Meanwhile, you can decorate the top with fresh strawberries, freeze-dried strawberries, roses and any other berries of your choice.

Store in an airtight container in your fridge for up to 3 to 4 days. Alternatively, freeze and defrost before serving.

Fruity Mango Cheezecake

A fresh and fruity cake. Adding vanilla and lime juice to mango really lifts the flavor, making it taste both fresh and creamy. Due to the high fruit content, I use a gelling agent to help set the cake and offset the liquid released by the fruits when blending.

MAKES ONE 8-INCH (20.5-CM) CAKE

CRUST

1½ cups (150 g) rolled oats (use gluten-free if required)

¼ cup (48 g) coconut sugar

¼ tsp Himalayan pink salt

2 tbsp (28 g) coconut oil (solid)

1½ tbsp (24 g) cashew butter

CHEEZECAKE FILLING

⅔ cup (97 g) cashews (dry weight)

2 fresh mangoes, cut into chunks

1 cup (240 ml) chilled coconut milk (using only the thick cream from the top of a 13.5-oz [400-ml] can)

¼ cup (60 ml) vanilla soy yogurt (substitute with plain soy or coconut yogurt plus 1 tsp vanilla extract)

½ cup (120 ml) maple syrup

2 tbsp (28 g) coconut oil (solid)

Juice of 1 lime

1¼ tsp (5 g) agar-agar

1 fresh mango, sliced, for garnish

1 cup (144 g) fresh strawberries, sliced, for garnish

Freeze-dried strawberries (optional), for garnish

Ahead of time, begin by preparing the cashews for the cheezecake filling. Soak the cashews in water for a minimum of 4 hours before rinsing with clean water and draining them, or quick soak in boiled water for 1 hour.

To make the crust, put the rolled oats, coconut sugar and salt in your food processor and blitz for 1 minute until it's a fine crumb consistency. Add the coconut oil and cashew butter and process for a couple more minutes, until the mixture starts to stick together and form a dough.

Line the bottom of an 8 x 4–inch (20.5 x 10.25–cm) cake pan with parchment paper and press the dough evenly into the bottom using a rubber spatula or the flat bottom of a glass. Once even, transfer the crust to the freezer while you prepare the next layer.

For the cheezecake, put the soaked cashews, mangoes, coconut milk, yogurt, maple syrup, coconut oil and lime juice in your high-speed blender. Blend the mixture on high speed until it's completely smooth and creamy.

Put the cheezecake mixture in a saucepan and bring to a simmer over medium heat. In a separate bowl, combine the agar-agar with 4 tablespoons (60 ml) of the cheezecake mix and whisk well. Add the agar-agar mixture to the saucepan and continue to simmer the mixture for 5 minutes, whisking continuously. Set aside to cool for 5 minutes.

Remove the crust from the freezer and pour the cheezecake mixture onto it, tapping the pan gently on your work surface to knock out any air bubbles. Place in the freezer to set for 6 hours or overnight.

Remove the cake from the pan while it's still frozen to keep the cheezecake from sticking to the edges. Decorate the top with sliced fresh mango, strawberries and freeze-dried strawberries, if desired.

Allow the cake to defrost for 45 minutes to 1 hour before serving.

Store in an airtight container in your fridge and consume in a couple of days. Alternatively, freeze and defrost before serving.

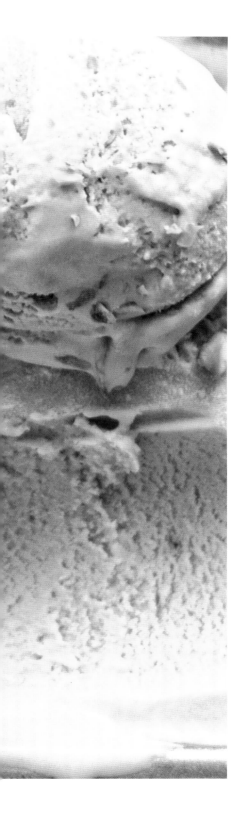

Ice Cream

It's summer and it's time to get out the ice cream maker! Just kidding—seasons are irrelevant when it comes to frozen desserts. Ice cream is by far my favorite dessert to enjoy, even if it's freezing outside! Getting an ice cream maker, although a small investment, has made such a difference to my homemade ice creams.

With these homemade ice cream recipes, you'll be able to make delicious, creamy ice cream from the comfort of your kitchen. These recipes will have you skipping the dairy aisle and store-bought desserts for good!

Coconut milk is the base for many cakes and ice creams; this creamy milk makes a great substitute for dairy. Most recipes will call for the coconut milk to be chilled first to separate the liquid from the thick creamy part. For this reason, I always keep a can or two in the fridge. To prepare your coconut milk, always use full fat, store the can in the fridge overnight and then scoop out the heavy cream from the top of the can.

Pistachio lovers, try the fragrant creamy Pistachio Ice Cream on page 83. For ice creams on the go, my Double Chocolate–Salted Caramel Ice Cream Bars (page 92) and Cookie Dough Ice Cream Bars (page 95) are the perfect indulgence.

"Vish Food" Salted Caramel and Chocolate Ice Cream

The most indulgent dessert you can imagine: creamy rich chocolate ice cream, dark chocolate chunks and a sweet sticky caramel sauce. This ice cream is really easy to make and doesn't require a blender or food processor, just a few bowls and an ice cream maker and you're good to go.

MAKES ONE 3¼-CUP (780-ML) TUB

ICE CREAM

2 (13.5-oz [400-ml]) cans chilled coconut milk (using only the thick cream from the top of the can)

1 cup (240 ml) oat milk or other plant-based milk

6 oz (170 g) vegan-friendly dark chocolate (I used 70 percent cacao)

1 tsp vanilla extract

¼ cup plus 2 tbsp (90 ml) maple syrup

STICKY CARAMEL SAUCE

1 cup (258 g) cashew butter

¾ cup (180 ml) maple syrup

½ tsp pink Himalayan salt

2 oz (57 g) vegan-friendly dark chocolate, chopped into small chunks, for garnish, divided

For the ice cream, put the coconut milk and oat milk in a saucepan and bring to a simmer over medium heat. Once simmering, remove the pan from the heat and stir in the chocolate. Whisk well until the mixture is smooth and the chocolate is melted without any lumps. Lastly, add the vanilla extract and maple syrup and whisk until smooth. Set aside to cool for about 30 minutes or until it comes to room temperature.

Once cooled, put the mixture in your ice cream maker and churn according to the manufacturer's instructions. (My ice cream maker takes about 40 minutes to churn.)

To prepare the sticky caramel sauce, put the cashew butter, maple syrup and salt in a large bowl. Whisk vigorously until the mixture is silky smooth. Set aside in the fridge while the ice cream is churning.

Once the ice cream has finished churning, put it in a large mixing bowl and very gently fold half of the caramel mixture through it using a rubber spatula. Be careful not to overmix, as the desired result is a marbled caramel effect.

Add about three-fourths of the dark chocolate chunks to the bowl and gently fold them into the ice cream. Transfer the ice cream to a loaf pan or lunch box, cover tightly with parchment paper and place in the freezer for 4 hours.

Remove the ice cream from the freezer 10 minutes before serving to allow it to thaw slightly. Drizzle with the remaining sticky caramel sauce and chocolate chunks.

Scoop the ice cream into serving dishes using a warm ice cream scoop and serve immediately.

Raspberry Ripple Ice Cream

A classic flavor that everyone loves. This ice cream has a vanilla-coconut milk and oat milk base and a tart, fruity raspberry sauce. The combination of creamy vanilla ice cream and fresh raspberry is one that never gets old.

MAKES ONE 3¼-CUP (780-ML) TUB

RASPBERRY SAUCE
¾ cup (188 g) frozen raspberries

2 tbsp (30 ml) maple syrup

ICE CREAM
2 (13.5-oz [400-ml]) cans chilled coconut milk (using only the thick cream from the top of the can)

1 cup (240 ml) oat milk

¾ cup (180 ml) maple syrup

2 tbsp (28 g) coconut oil (solid)

1 tsp vanilla bean paste

¼ tsp almond extract

Begin by preparing the raspberry sauce. Put the raspberries in a saucepan and allow them to defrost for 30 minutes before bringing them to a simmer for 10 minutes over medium heat. Pass the mixture through a fine-mesh sieve, discard the seeds and add the liquid back to the saucepan. Add the maple syrup and simmer for another 5 minutes, stirring continuously. Set the sauce aside to cool while you prepare the ice cream.

For the ice cream, put all of the ice cream ingredients in your high-speed blender and blitz for a few minutes until smooth and creamy. Transfer the mixture to your ice cream maker and churn according to the manufacturer's instructions (about 40 minutes).

Once the ice cream has finished churning, transfer it to a large bowl and carefully fold in three-fourths of the raspberry sauce using a rubber spatula. Transfer the ice cream to a loaf pan and top with the remaining raspberry sauce, then use a knife to create a swirl effect on the top.

Cover the pan and freeze for a minimum of 4 hours or until the ice cream is set.

To serve, remove the ice cream from the freezer 10 minutes ahead of time and use a warm ice cream scoop to serve.

Vanilla Bean and Chamomile Ice Cream   *Gluten-Free*

This recipe is a twist on classic vanilla ice cream that includes a hint of delicate floral chamomile tea. The cashews add a rich and creamy consistency to the ice cream and it can be enjoyed as "soft serve" straight from the ice cream machine.

MAKES ONE 3¼-CUP (780-ML) TUB

1½ cups (219 g) cashews (dry weight)

3 tbsp (14 g) loose chamomile tea

3 tbsp (45 ml) boiling water

1 vanilla pod

1 (13.5-oz [400-ml]) can chilled coconut milk (using only the thick cream from the top of the can)

¾ cup (180 ml) maple syrup

3 tbsp (42 g) coconut oil (solid)

Pinch of Himalayan pink salt

Ahead of time, prepare the cashews. Soak them in water for a minimum of 4 hours before rinsing with clean water and draining them, or quick soak in boiled water for 1 hour.

Next, put the chamomile tea and boiling water in a cup and allow to steep for 5 minutes.

Cut the vanilla pod from top to bottom and scrape out the seeds using the back of your knife. Put the vanilla seeds and vanilla pod in a saucepan along with the coconut milk and chamomile tea mixture. Bring the mixture to a simmer and allow to cook for 5 minutes to infuse.

Pass the mixture through a fine-mesh sieve to remove the vanilla pod and chamomile flowers and put the remaining liquid into a high-speed blender. Add the cashews, maple syrup, coconut oil and salt to the blender and blitz for 5 minutes until smooth and creamy. Transfer the mixture to a large bowl and refrigerate for 20 minutes to cool.

Once cooled completely, put the mixture in your ice cream maker and churn for 40 minutes or according to the manufacturer's instructions. Once thick and creamy, transfer the ice cream to a loaf pan lined with parchment paper and cover tightly with more parchment paper or some plastic wrap.

Freeze the ice cream for at least 4 hours before serving.

Hunnycomb Ice Cream   *Gluten-Free*

I use aquafaba, which is the liquid from canned chickpeas, as the base for this ice cream recipe. Sounds gross? I thought so, too, but don't worry. It's completely flavorless once incorporated into the recipe. When whisked, aquafaba has a soft meringue consistency and it's perfect for adding a fluffy, airy texture to your ice cream. This recipe makes extra "hunnycomb"—any leftovers can be stored in an airtight container at room temperature, so you can enjoy it alongside ice cream, dipped in dairy-free chocolate or simply on its own!

MAKES ONE 3¼-CUP (780-ML) TUB

HUNNYCOMB

Sunflower oil, for greasing

¼ cup (60 ml) water

1½ cups (180 g) caster sugar

⅓ cup (80 ml) golden syrup

1½ tsp (7 g) baking soda

ICE CREAM

½ cup (120 ml) aquafaba
(the liquid part from canned chickpeas; chill the can overnight and strain)

½ tsp cream of tartar

2 (13.5-oz [400-ml]) cans chilled coconut milk (using only the thick cream from the can)

½ cup (120 ml) maple syrup

2 tsp (10 ml) vanilla extract

Pinch of salt

For the hunnycomb, begin by making sure you have all your equipment ready and ingredients measured out, as you will need to work quickly once the mixture is ready.

Line a large baking dish with parchment paper before oiling it with a small amount of sunflower oil.

Put the water, sugar and golden syrup in a large saucepan and place over medium heat. Stir using a wooden spoon for a few minutes until all of the sugar has melted.

At this point, stop stirring the mixture, as continuing to do so will cause the sugar to crystallize. Turn up the heat to medium-high and insert a candy thermometer into the syrup to monitor the temperature. You want the syrup to get to 300°F (149°C), known as the "hard crack" stage of candy making. This will take around 15 minutes, so be patient and keep a very close eye on the saucepan.

Once the syrup hits 300°F (149°C), remove the saucepan from the heat and immediately add in the baking soda. Whisk well to combine the mixture (being very careful not to touch it, as it is extremely hot!). Transfer the mixture directly to your baking dish and do not touch it once filled.

Allow the hunnycomb to set completely for 1 to 2 hours without moving it. Once it is completely set and at room temperature, remove the hunnycomb from the dish and cut it into small pieces.

For the ice cream, begin by putting the aquafaba and cream of tartar in a large bowl. Use an electric handheld whisk or stand mixer to beat the mixture for 10 minutes, until soft peaks form.

(continued)

Hunnycomb Ice Cream (continued)

Put the coconut milk, maple syrup, vanilla extract and salt in your high-speed blender and blitz until smooth. Carefully add the coconut milk mixture to the whipped aquafaba, ½ cup (120 ml) at a time, folding it gently through each time. Continue until the entire mixture is incorporated, being careful not to overmix it as you want to keep those airy bubbles.

Transfer the mixture to your ice cream maker and churn for 40 minutes or until ready based on the manufacturer's instructions.

Transfer the ice cream mixture to a large bowl and add half of the chopped hunny-comb, carefully folding it through with a rubber spatula. Transfer the ice cream to a loaf pan and top with some more of the chopped hunnycomb pieces. (Any leftover hunnycomb can be stored in an airtight container at room temperature.) Put the ice cream in the freezer to set for a minimum of 4 hours or overnight.

Remove the ice cream from the freezer about 5 minutes before you plan on eating it. Use an ice cream scoop dipped in hot water to serve.

Pistachio Ice Cream   *Gluten-Free*

Pistachio ice cream has got to be one of my favorite flavors. It was a rare find growing up in Ireland, so I would always jump at the opportunity to try some. I attempted to make my first homemade version in my teens—years later this veganized version is better than any that I can remember, homemade or store-bought. The pistachios in this recipe not only give a beautiful color and fragrant flavor, they also give the ice cream a wonderful thick and creamy texture that rivals any gelato.

MAKES ONE 3¼-CUP (780-ML) TUB

ICE CREAM

1 cup (123 g) shelled pistachios

2 (13.5-oz [400-ml]) cans chilled coconut milk (using only the thick cream from the top of the can)

1 cup (240 ml) maple syrup

3 tbsp (42 g) coconut oil (solid)

½ tsp almond extract

2 tsp (10 ml) vanilla extract

1 tbsp (8 g) wheatgrass powder (optional, for color)

TOPPING

¼ cup (31 g) chopped pistachios

Ahead of time, prepare the shelled pistachios by soaking them. Put them in a large bowl and cover with water for at least 2 hours. Rinse the pistachios with clean water and remove as much of the skin as possible. They should come off easily using your fingers, as the water will have loosened them.

Put all of the ice cream ingredients in your high-speed blender and blitz for a few minutes until smooth and creamy. Make sure there are no lumps in the mixture. Transfer the mixture to your ice cream maker and churn based on the manufacturer's instructions. (Mine takes about 40 minutes for the ice cream to get thick.)

Transfer the ice cream to a loaf pan and top with the chopped pistachios. Cover the pan and freeze for a minimum of 4 hours, or until the ice cream is set.

To serve, remove the ice cream from the freezer 10 minutes ahead of time and use a warm ice cream scoop to serve.

See image on page 72.

Boozy Tiramisu Ice Cream

Gluten-Free

This dessert combines the best of both dessert worlds: ice cream and tiramisu! Not only does the dark rum give this ice cream a delicious boozy flavor, it also helps to keep the ice cream at a scoopable texture.

MAKES ONE 1-QUART (1-L) TUB

ICE CREAM

1 cup (146 g) cashews (dry weight)

2 tbsp (30 ml) boiling water

3 tbsp (30 g) instant coffee granules

2 (13.5-oz [400-ml]) cans chilled coconut milk (using only the thick cream from the top of the can)

½ cup (96 g) coconut sugar

½ cup (120 ml) maple syrup

½ cup (120 ml) vanilla soy yogurt (use plain soy or coconut yogurt if preferred)

3 tbsp (42 g) coconut oil (solid)

1 tsp vanilla extract

1 tbsp (15 ml) dark rum or 1 tsp rum essence

CHOCOLATE SAUCE

¼ cup (60 ml) vanilla soy yogurt (use plain soy or coconut yogurt if preferred)

3 tbsp (47 g) cashew butter

3 tbsp (45 ml) maple syrup

1 tbsp (5 g) cacao powder

RUM DOUGH BALLS

¾ cup (109 g) cashews

⅛ tsp Himalayan pink salt

4 Medjool dates, pitted

1 tbsp (15 ml) dark rum

Coffee beans, for garnish

Ahead of time, start by soaking the cashews for the ice cream base in water for a minimum of 4 hours before rinsing with clean water and draining them, or quick soak in boiled water for 1 hour.

Mix the boiling water and coffee granules in a cup. Put the coffee shot in your high-speed blender along with the rest of the ice cream ingredients and blitz for 5 minutes or until the mixture is smooth and creamy.

Make sure the mixture is completely cool before you transfer it to your ice cream maker. Churn for a total of 40 minutes or according to the manufacturer's instructions.

While your ice cream is churning, make the chocolate sauce. Put all the sauce ingredients in a bowl and whisk until smooth. Set aside.

For the rum dough balls, put the unsoaked cashews and salt in a food processor and blitz to a crumb consistency. Add the dates and rum and blitz further until a sticky dough is formed. Set aside about a quarter of the mixture to crumble on top of the ice cream later. Roll the remaining dough into small balls between the palms of your hands.

Once the ice cream is thick and has finished churning, transfer it to a large bowl. Gently fold in the rum dough balls using a rubber spatula. Next, fold in about half of the chocolate sauce.

Transfer the ice cream to a loaf pan lined with parchment paper and top with the remaining sauce, rum dough crumble and a scattering of coffee beans, if desired.

Cover the ice cream tightly with parchment paper and freeze for 4 hours before serving.

Strawberry Cheezecake Ice Cream   *Gluten-Free*

This recipe is perfect for both ice cream and cheesecake lovers. The cashews form the base of the ice cream, which, with a hint of fresh lemon juice, give it a tangy cheesecake flavor. The result is a creamy ice cream with a sweet and fruity strawberry sauce and doughy cashew pieces.

MAKES ONE 3¼-CUP (780-ML) TUB

STRAWBERRY SAUCE

1 cup (144 g) frozen strawberries

⅓ cup (80 ml) apple juice

1 tbsp (15 ml) maple syrup

1 tbsp (8 g) cornstarch

CHEEZECAKE ICE CREAM

1½ cups (219 g) cashews (dry weight)

1 (13.5-oz [400-ml]) can chilled coconut milk (using only the thick cream from the top of the can)

⅓ cup (80 ml) vanilla soy yogurt (or plain soy yogurt plus 1 tsp vanilla bean paste)

¾ cup (180 ml) maple syrup

¼ cup (56 g) coconut oil (solid)

1 tbsp (15 ml) lemon juice

5 fresh strawberries, cut into small cubes

CASHEW CRUMBLE

⅓ cup (49 g) cashews

¼ cup (24 g) almond flour or ground almonds

Pinch of Himalayan pink salt

1 tbsp (15 ml) maple syrup

Ahead of time, prepare the cashews for the ice cream. Soak them in water for a minimum of 4 hours before rinsing with clean water and draining them, or quick soak in boiled water for 1 hour.

For the sauce, put the frozen strawberries and apple juice in a saucepan and bring to a simmer over medium-high heat. Cook for 15 to 20 minutes, until the strawberries have broken down and the mixture has a thick consistency. Add the maple syrup, sift the cornstarch into the mixture and cook for another 2 minutes, whisking continuously to ensure it doesn't burn. Set the sauce aside to cool for 20 minutes.

Meanwhile, prepare the ice cream by putting the soaked cashews, coconut milk, yogurt, maple syrup, coconut oil and lemon juice in a high-speed blender. Blitz for 5 minutes or until the mixture is smooth and creamy.

Transfer the mixture to your ice cream maker and churn for a total of 40 minutes or according to the manufacturer's instructions. After about 10 minutes of churning, add the chopped strawberry pieces to the ice cream machine.

While your ice cream is churning, make the cashew crumble by putting the unsoaked cashews in a food processor and blitzing them to a crumb consistency. Add the almond flour, salt and maple syrup and blend further for a minute, until the mixture sticks together between your fingers. Separate out one-third of the dough and reserve to garnish the top of the ice cream. Form small dough balls with the remaining cashew crumbs and add them to the ice cream maker with the churning ice cream.

Once the ice cream is thick and has finished churning, add three-fourths of the strawberry sauce to the ice cream maker and allow it to mix for about 30 seconds. Transfer the ice cream to a loaf pan lined with parchment paper and top with the remaining sauce and reserved cashew crumbs.

Cover the ice cream tightly with parchment paper and freeze for 4 hours before serving.

Choc Chunk Cherry Ice Cream

If you love cherries, this ice cream was made for you. The almond extract enhances the cherry flavor to bring it to the next level. This ice cream is thick and creamy, while being fruity and chocolatey all at the same time.

MAKES ONE 1-QUART (1-L) TUB

CHERRY ICE CREAM

⅔ cup (97 g) cashews (dry weight)

2 (13.5-oz [400-ml]) cans chilled coconut milk (using only the thick cream from the top of the can)

¼ cup (56 g) coconut oil (solid)

1 cup (240 ml) maple syrup

2 tsp (10 ml) vanilla extract

1 tsp almond extract

2⅛ cups (330 g) frozen cherries, defrosted and strained (reserve the juice and half of the cherries for the sauce)

2 oz (57 g) chopped vegan-friendly dark chocolate

CHERRY SAUCE

½ cup (120 ml) cherry juice (reserved from above)

2 tbsp (16 g) cornstarch

½ cup (120 ml) water

¼ cup (60 ml) maple syrup

1 generous cup (155 g) defrosted cherries (reserved from above)

1.5 oz (42 g) chopped vegan-friendly dark chocolate, for garnish

Fresh cherries, for garnish

Ahead of time, prepare the cashews for the ice cream by soaking them in water for a minimum of 4 hours before rinsing with clean water and draining them, or quick soak in boiled water for 1 hour.

Prepare the ice cream by putting the soaked cashews, coconut milk, coconut oil, maple syrup, vanilla extract and almond extract in a high-speed blender. Add 1 cup plus 2 tablespoons (175 g) of the defrosted cherries and blitz for 5 minutes, or until smooth and creamy.

Transfer the mixture to your ice cream maker and churn for a total of 40 minutes or according to the manufacturer's instructions. After about 10 minutes of churning, add the chopped dark chocolate chunks to the ice cream machine.

While your ice cream is churning, make the cherry sauce. Put the cherry juice and cornstarch in a small bowl and whisk until all the lumps are gone. Add the water, maple syrup and cornstarch mixture to a saucepan and bring to a simmer. Cook for 5 minutes while whisking continuously. Remove the pan from the heat and stir in 1 generous cup (155 g) of defrosted cherries. Set the mixture aside to cool.

Once the ice cream is thick and has finished churning, transfer it to a large bowl. Gently fold in about three-fourths of the cooled cherry sauce using a rubber spatula. Transfer the ice cream to a loaf pan lined with parchment paper and top with the remaining sauce and chocolate chunks. Cover the ice cream tightly with parchment paper and freeze for 4 hours.

Serve topped with fresh cherries.

Cinnamon-Blueberry Ice Cream

Gluten-Free

This ice cream is perfect for summer or winter, as it's got summery berries and wintry spice!
I find that adding cinnamon to blueberries really enhances and complements their flavor.
Top tip: Use small blueberries (or the wild variety), as they have a stronger color and taste.

MAKES ONE 1-QUART (1-L) TUB

⅔ cup (97 g) cashews (dry weight)

1 cup (155 g) frozen wild blueberries, defrosted

2 (13.5-oz [400-ml]) cans chilled coconut milk (using only the thick cream from the top of the can)

1 cup (240 ml) maple syrup

2 tbsp (28 g) coconut oil (solid)

1 tsp vanilla bean paste

2½ tsp (6 g) ground cinnamon

Ahead of time, soak the cashews in water for a minimum of 4 hours before rinsing with clean water and draining them, or quick soak in boiled water for 1 hour.

Put all of the ingredients in a high-speed blender and blitz until smooth and creamy, a few minutes.

Transfer the mixture to your ice cream machine and churn based on the manufacturer's instructions; mine takes about 40 minutes for the ice cream to get thick.

Once the ice cream has finished churning, transfer it to a large loaf pan or freezable container of your choice. Cover the pan with additional parchment paper and freeze for a minimum of 4 hours, or until the ice cream is set.

To serve, remove the ice cream from the freezer 10 minutes ahead of time and use a warm ice cream scoop to serve.

Double Chocolate-Salted Caramel Ice Cream Bars *Gluten-Free*

These ice cream bars are pure indulgence, with creamy chocolate ice cream and silky rich salted caramel encased in a chocolate shell. They are really easy to make, but are sure to impress the pickiest of eaters! In fact, I recommend doubling up on the recipe if you've got spare molds, because they are guaranteed to disappear fast. The molds I use for this are "magnum"-shaped ice cream molds, 3½ x 2 x 1 inches (89 x 51 x 25.5 mm) in size, holding 6 tablespoons (90 ml) each.

MAKES 4 BARS

SALTED CARAMEL
¼ cup (60 ml) maple syrup

2 tbsp (31 g) cashew butter

1 tbsp (9 g) maca powder

¼ tsp Himalayan pink salt

ICE CREAM
⅓ cup (49 g) cashews (dry weight)

1 cup (240 ml) chilled coconut milk (using only the thick cream from the top of a 13.5-oz [400-ml] can)

¼ cup (60 ml) maple syrup

2 tbsp (31 g) cashew butter

1½ tbsp (8 g) cacao powder

COATING
3.75 oz (106 g) vegan-friendly chocolate (homemade Mylk Chocolate with Cashews and Lucuma on page 124)

Coconut sugar, for garnish

Ahead of time, prepare the cashews for the ice cream by soaking them in water for a minimum of 4 hours before rinsing with clean water and draining them, or quick soak in boiled water for 1 hour.

To make the salted caramel, put all of the caramel ingredients in a bowl and whisk until smooth. Into each of four ice cream–shaped silicone molds, spoon 1½ tablespoons (22 ml) of the caramel. Set aside.

For the ice cream, put all of the ice cream ingredients (including the soaked cashews) in your high-speed blender and blitz until smooth and creamy. Pour the ice cream into the silicone molds on top of the caramel. Insert an ice cream stick into each mold. Place in the freezer to set for 6 hours or overnight.

Melt the chocolate in a double boiler over simmering water. Remove the ice cream bars from the molds and spoon the melted chocolate over each one until fully coated. Put the ice cream bars on a sheet of parchment paper while they set, which they can do on the counter if the treats were solidly frozen.

To garnish, drizzle a little more melted chocolate over each ice cream bar and sprinkle with coconut sugar.

Serve immediately or store in the freezer for up to 1 month.

Cookie Dough Ice Cream Bars

There's nothing quite as good as a fully edible ice cream bar; no stick, no spoon, just a big cookie sandwich stuffed with creamy vanilla ice cream. This recipe makes a big batch of ice cream bars, which are perfect to keep as your go-to stash in the freezer when you're craving something sweet.

MAKES 9 TO 12 BARS

COOKIE DOUGH

2 cups (200 g) rolled oats (use gluten-free if required)

2 cups (192 g) almond flour or ground almonds

½ cup (96 g) coconut sugar

¼ tsp Himalayan pink salt

3 tbsp (47 g) almond butter or cashew butter

1 tbsp (14 g) coconut oil (solid)

1 tsp vanilla extract

¼ cup plus 1 tbsp (75 ml) almond milk

8 oz (226 g) vegan-friendly chocolate or homemade Mylk Chocolate with Cashews and Lucuma (page 124), cut into small chunks

VANILLA ICE CREAM

1 cup (146 g) cashews (dry weight)

1 (13.5-oz [400-ml]) can chilled coconut milk (using only the thick cream from the top of the can)

½ cup (120 ml) almond milk

½ cup (120 ml) maple syrup

1 tsp vanilla bean paste

2 tbsp (15 g) lucuma powder

⅛ tsp Himalayan pink salt

¼ tsp ground cinnamon

Ahead of time, prepare the cashews for the ice cream by soaking them in water for a minimum of 4 hours before rinsing with clean water and draining them, or quick soak in boiled water for 1 hour.

To make the cookie dough, put the rolled oats, almond flour, coconut sugar and salt in a food processor and blitz to a fine crumb consistency. Add the almond or cashew butter, coconut oil, vanilla extract and almond milk and blend again until everything sticks together to form a dough.

Transfer the dough to a large bowl and add the chocolate chunks. Use your hands to knead the dough until the chocolate chunks are mixed in evenly.

Split the mixture into two halves. Roll out each half between two sheets of parchment paper until they fit the size of your baking dish or tray, 11 x 7 inches (28 x 18 cm) or similar.

Line the bottom of the dish with parchment paper and place one sheet of the cookie dough into it as the base. Gently wrap the other sheet of cookie dough in parchment, place it on a tray and put it in the freezer.

For the ice cream, put all of the ice cream ingredients in your high-speed blender and blend until smooth and creamy. Pour the ice cream into the dish on top of the first sheet of cookie dough. Transfer to the freezer to set.

After about 2 hours, check that the ice cream layer has set and place the second sheet of cookie dough on top of it. Cover and freeze for another 4 hours or overnight.

Once ready, remove the ice cream block from the dish and cut into squares. It will make between 9 and 12 bars, depending on the size into which you cut the portions.

Serve immediately or store in the freezer for up to 1 month.

Cookies and Brownies

Every kitchen needs a stash of delicious treats ready for when friends or family come around. No-bake cookies and brownies are some of the simplest recipes you can make to satisfy a sweet tooth.

Everyone loves a good cookie dough, and cookies made with plant-based ingredients can be eaten straight from the bowl, unlike the ones that contain eggs.

From Triple Chocolate Brownies (page 105) to White Chocolate and Strawberry Blondies (page 106), Chocolate Chip Cookies (page 102) to Peanut Butter Cookies (page 98), these recipes take very little time and effort to put together but don't compromise on texture or taste.

Peanut Butter Cookies

This no-bake recipe is a fuss-free way to make delicious, crumbly cookies that have an intense peanut butter flavor without having to even turn on the oven! Once ready, try dipping them in chocolate for a delicious twist on this classic flavor.

MAKES 15 TO 20 COOKIES

COOKIES

¾ cup (126 g) roasted buckwheat or raw buckwheat toasted according to instructions (see page 21)

2 cups (180 g) oat flour (use gluten-free if required, see Note)

¼ tsp salt

Pinch of ground cinnamon

¾ cup (194 g) crunchy peanut butter

½ cup (120 ml) maple syrup

1 tbsp (15 ml) almond milk

Roasted salted peanuts, chopped, for garnish

Peanut butter, for garnish

Put the buckwheat in your food processor and pulse until it forms a flour-like consistency. Transfer the buckwheat flour to a large bowl. Add the oat flour, salt and cinnamon to the bowl and stir to make sure everything is evenly mixed.

In a separate bowl, combine the crunchy peanut butter, maple syrup and almond milk. Whisk the mixture until smooth and pour it into the large bowl along with the dry ingredients.

Using a rubber spatula, bring the mixture together before using your hands to knead the dough and make sure everything is evenly mixed.

Place the dough between two sheets of parchment paper and use a rolling pin to roll it out to approximately ½ inch (1.25 cm) in thickness. Use a 2-inch (5-cm) cookie cutter to cut cookies or you can use a larger-sized cutter if preferred and make fewer cookies.

Set the cookies aside in the fridge to set for 1 hour and garnish with some peanuts and a drizzle of peanut butter before serving.

Store in an airtight container in the fridge for up to 1 week.

Note: To make your own oat flour from scratch, simply blend the rolled oats until finely ground.

White Chocolate, Macadamia and Pistachio Cookies

These nutty no-bake cookies are easy to make and are complemented by subtle flavors of tahini, coconut sugar and vanilla bean. You can make this recipe using my homemade White Chocolate with Vanilla and Lucuma recipe from page 128, or just grab vegan-friendly white chocolate if you prefer.

MAKES 10 TO 15 COOKIES

COOKIES

3.75 oz (106 g) vegan-friendly white chocolate (or homemade White Chocolate with Vanilla and Lucuma, page 128)

¼ cup (31 g) unsalted shelled pistachios, roughly chopped

⅓ cup (49 g) macadamia nuts, roughly chopped

2 cups (200 g) rolled oats (use gluten-free if required)

½ cup (96 g) coconut sugar (see Note)

¼ tsp Himalayan pink salt

⅓ cup (86 g) cashew butter

1 tsp vanilla bean paste

1 tbsp (15 ml) tahini

¼ cup (60 ml) vanilla soy milk

TOPPING

2 oz (57 g) chopped white chocolate (see page 128)

Note: Coconut sugar, a.k.a. coconut palm sugar, has a deep caramel flavor and has a similar sweetness to brown table sugar, but is less processed than refined sugars. I love to use this for cookie bases and biscuity crusts. It's also my preferred sweetener for chocolate, as liquid sweeteners tend to mess with the consistency.

For the cookie dough, chop the white chocolate, pistachios and macadamia nuts into small chunks, add to a bowl and set aside in the freezer. This will make the chocolate more stable when you're adding it to the cookie dough and will prevent it from melting.

Put the rolled oats, coconut sugar and salt in your food processor and blitz for a couple of minutes, until they reach a flour-like consistency. Transfer the mixture to a large bowl and set aside.

In a separate smaller bowl, prepare the wet ingredients. Put the cashew butter, vanilla bean paste, tahini and vanilla soy milk in the bowl and whisk until the ingredients form a smooth paste. Add the paste to the large bowl with the dry ingredients and use a rubber spatula to bring the mixture together before kneading with your hands to make sure the dough is evenly mixed.

Add the chopped white chocolate, pistachios and macadamia chunks to the dough and continue to knead until they are mixed evenly throughout the dough.

Use an ice cream scoop to measure out the individual cookies, pressing the cookie dough firmly into the scoop before setting the cookies on a baking sheet lined with parchment paper. Repeat this for the remaining cookie dough and use a fork to press down on and shape the cookies.

Place the cookies in the freezer to set for 1 hour.

Meanwhile, melt the white chocolate for the garnish in a double boiler over simmering water. Dip one half of each cookie in the melted chocolate and place them on a cooling rack or baking tray lined with parchment paper to set.

Once set, you can store them in the fridge in an airtight container for up to 1 week.

Chocolate Chip Cookies

These no-bake cookies are probably the easiest chocolate chip cookies you will ever make! They are made in a bowl and don't require any equipment such as a food processor, blender or oven. It's a win-win because they have all the great taste with minimal effort.

MAKES 12 COOKIES

2 cups (180 g) oat flour (use gluten-free if required)

¾ cup (72 g) almond flour or ground almonds

½ tsp Himalayan pink salt

½ cup (129 g) cashew butter

½ cup (120 ml) maple syrup

2 tsp (10 ml) vanilla extract

¾ cup (126 g) vegan-friendly chocolate chips

In a large bowl, combine the oat flour, almond flour and salt. Whisk the mixture to make sure everything is evenly mixed.

In a separate bowl, combine the cashew butter, maple syrup and vanilla extract. Whisk well, until the ingredients form a paste. Transfer the paste to the bowl with the dry ingredients and use a rubber spatula to bring the mixture together to form a dough, or you can also use your hands to knead the dough together at this point.

Lastly, add the chocolate chips to the bowl and work them through the dough with your hands. Try to make sure that the chocolate chips are distributed as evenly as possible throughout the mixture. Form a large ball with the dough, cover and refrigerate for 1 hour.

Line a baking sheet with parchment paper and use an ice cream scoop to measure out the cookies. Place the cookies on the tray and use a fork to make a crisscross design on top of each one.

Transfer the cookies to an airtight container and refrigerate for up to 1 week.

Triple Chocolate Brownies   *Gluten-Free*

No-bake brownies are my favorite kind of brownies to make, as they are so simple and rich. They were the very first no-bake recipe that I tried, and since then I've probably made them a hundred times, with lots of different variations. Being no-bake means you can switch up some of the ingredients to suit your taste without messing up the recipe! I love trying out different nut butters to switch things up.

MAKES 12 BROWNIES

2 cups (234 g) walnuts

¼ cup (22 g) cacao powder

¼ tsp Himalayan pink salt

8 Medjool dates, pitted

2 tbsp (31 g) almond butter

½ tsp vanilla bean paste

2 oz (57 g) vegan-friendly white chocolate, such as homemade White Chocolate with Vanilla and Lucuma (page 128)

2 oz (57 g) vegan-friendly milk or dark chocolate, such as homemade Mylk Chocolate with Cashews and Lucuma (page 124)

12 pecans

Put the walnuts, cacao powder and salt in your food processor and pulse until they form a light crumb consistency. Add the Medjool dates, almond butter and vanilla bean paste and blend until the mixture forms a dough consistency.

Roughly chop the chocolates into chunks and add them to the food processor. Pulse for 30 seconds to combine them into the brownie dough. The mixture should stick together like a dough when you squeeze it between your fingers.

Transfer the brownie dough to your work surface, place between two sheets of parchment paper and roll out the dough to approximately ¾-inch (2-cm) thickness. Alternatively, you can transfer the dough to a 6½ x 6½–inch (16.5 x 16.5–cm) baking dish lined with parchment paper and press it down evenly into the dish using a rubber spatula.

Top with pecans and transfer the dish to the fridge for 1 hour before cutting the brownies into 12 portions.

Store the brownies in the fridge in an airtight container for up to 5 days.

White Chocolate and Strawberry Blondies

If you're looking for a summery version of no-bake brownies that's just as easy, then this recipe is for you. Freeze-dried strawberries add a sweet-and-fruity twist to these no-bake treats.

MAKES 16 SMALL BLONDIES

1½ cups (135 g) oat flour (use gluten-free if required)

1 cup (96 g) almond flour or ground almonds

½ tsp Himalayan pink salt

½ cup (120 ml) maple syrup

½ cup (129 g) almond butter

1 tsp vanilla extract

¼ cup (5 g) freeze-dried strawberries

4 oz (113 g) chopped vegan-friendly white chocolate (see page 128)

Put the oat flour, almond flour and salt in a large bowl and stir well. In a separate smaller bowl, combine the maple syrup, almond butter and vanilla extract by whisking them into a smooth paste.

Transfer the paste to the bowl with the dry ingredients and use a rubber spatula to bring the mixture together to form a dough. Use your hands to knead the dough and make sure the ingredients are evenly combined.

Lastly, add the freeze-dried strawberries and chopped white chocolate to the bowl and mix them through the dough until evenly distributed. Form the dough into a large ball, cover and refrigerate for 1 hour.

Place the dough between two sheets of parchment paper and use a rolling pin to roll it out to approximately ¾ inch (2 cm) in thickness.

Cut the blondies into 16 portions and store them refrigerated in an airtight container for up to 5 days.

Cupcakes and Donuts

Think classic flavor combinations served in a less-conventional form. One of the best parts of visiting a donut or cupcake shop is the array of flavors and varieties on display. Cupcakes and donuts are an exciting way to combine your favorite sweet flavor combos into one snack.

From banoffee cupcakes with layers of salted caramel, sweet banana and coconut cream (page 113) to pumpkin spice donuts with a coffee kick (page 121), these easy-to-make recipes are perfect for taking with you on the go to have with your tea or coffee.

Strawberry Surprise Cupcakes

The combination of strawberries and cream in these fruity, fancy little cupcakes is a perfect match. Inside each jam-filled cupcake is a whole strawberry encased in coconut cream. These cupcakes are made from wholesome ingredients and can be enjoyed as a snack or a healthier alternative to store-bought cupcakes.

MAKES 6 CUPCAKES

CREAM TOPPING

1 (13.5-oz [400-m]) can chilled coconut milk (using only the thick cream from the top of the can)

2 tbsp (30 ml) maple syrup

½ tsp vanilla bean paste

BASE

1 cup (100 g) rolled oats (use gluten-free if required)

½ cup (47 g) dried shredded coconut

¼ cup (5 g) freeze-dried strawberry pieces or strawberry powder

⅛ tsp Himalayan pink salt

5 Medjool dates, pitted

½ tsp vanilla bean paste

FILLING

¼ cup (60 ml) strawberry jam, such as homemade Strawberry and Vanilla Bean Jam (page 152)

6 fresh strawberries

Freeze-dried strawberries, for garnish

For the cream, put all of the cream topping ingredients in a large bowl and beat with an electric mixer until smooth and thick. Transfer the cream to a large piping bag fitted with an open star tip. Secure the top of the piping bag with an elastic band and place in the fridge to chill for 1 hour.

To make the base, put the rolled oats, dried coconut, freeze-dried strawberries and salt in your food processor and blitz to a fine flour consistency. Add the dates and the vanilla bean paste and blend further for a minute until they form a dough.

Separate the dough into six parts and roll them into balls. Place the balls into a cupcake tray lined with paper muffin cups and press down into the center of each dough ball to create a hole in the middle.

To assemble the cupcakes, put 2 teaspoons (10 ml) of the jam into the center of each cupcake. Cut the tops off the strawberries and place one strawberry into each cupcake on top of the jam. Pipe the coconut cream around each strawberry to top the cupcakes. Finish by sprinkling some freeze-dried strawberry pieces on top.

Keep these cupcakes stored in the fridge in an airtight container. Because they contain fresh strawberries, they are best consumed fresh on the same day they are made, but will keep for a couple of days.

Banoffee Cupcakes

These cupcakes are an easy way to enjoy all the flavors and texture of traditional banoffee pie in a plant-based version made from wholesome ingredients. They are filled with a favorite surprise of mine: sweet maca caramel sauce, which you can add more or less of depending on the level of sweetness you want.

MAKES 8 CUPCAKES

CREAM TOPPING

1 (13.5-oz [400-ml]) can chilled coconut milk (using only the thick cream from the top of the can)

1 tbsp (15 ml) maple syrup

1 tsp vanilla extract

BASE

½ cup (59 g) walnuts

1 cup (100 g) rolled oats (use gluten-free if required)

½ cup (48 g) almond flour or ground almonds

⅛ tsp Himalayan pink salt

1 Medjool date, pitted

1 small banana

FILLING

2 tbsp plus 2 tsp (40 ml) Salted Maca Caramel (see page 155)

Grated vegan-friendly dark chocolate, for garnish

½ banana, sliced, for garnish

Juice of ½ lemon, for garnish

For the cream, put all of the topping ingredients in a large bowl and beat with an electric mixer until smooth and thick. Transfer the cream to a large piping bag fitted with an open star tip. Secure the top of the piping bag with an elastic band and place in the fridge to chill for 1 hour.

To make the base, put the walnuts, rolled oats, almond flour and salt in your food processor and blitz to a fine flour consistency. Add the date and the banana and blend further for a minute until they form a dough.

Separate the dough into eight parts and roll them into balls. Place the balls into a cupcake tray lined with paper muffin cups and press down into the center of each dough ball to create a hole in the middle.

Place a teaspoon of the maca caramel into the center of each cupcake. Pipe the coconut cream on top of each cupcake and sprinkle with grated dark chocolate.

Put the banana slices in a bowl with the lemon juice and turn them to coat them fully in the juice. This will prevent the banana from discoloring. Place the banana slices on some paper towels or a clean kitchen towel to remove any excess liquid and use them to decorate the tops of the cupcakes.

Keep these cupcakes stored in the fridge in an airtight container for up to 2 to 3 days.

Cherry "No-Bakewells"   *Gluten-Free*

Chances are if you grew up in Ireland or the UK, you will have grown up eating these buns.
The frangipani filling tastes like marzipan, which is a great addition to cherry desserts.
The lemon icing on these cupcakes makes them super sweet, like the original version,
but feel free to cut back on the amount of icing or omit it completely if you're avoiding
refined sugar.

MAKES 6 CUPCAKES

CRUST

Coconut oil or olive oil, for greasing

2 cups (192 g) almond flour or ground almonds, plus extra for dusting

¼ cup (48 g) coconut sugar

⅛ tsp Himalayan pink salt

2½ tbsp (35 g) coconut oil (solid)

½ tsp water

CHERRY JAM

1 cup (154 g) cherries, pitted and halved

¼ cup (60 ml) water

¼ cup (60 ml) maple syrup

1 tsp cornstarch

FRANGIPANI FILLING

½ cup (48 g) almond flour or ground almonds

3 tbsp (45 ml) maple syrup

1 tsp almond extract

1 tsp vanilla extract

LEMON ICING

1 cup (120 g) icing sugar

Juice of ½ lemon

½ tsp vanilla extract

2 tbsp (30 ml) almond milk

1 tbsp (14 g) coconut oil (solid)

6 fresh cherries, for garnish

To prepare your muffin tins and prevent the cupcakes from sticking, use some coconut oil or olive oil to grease six compartments of a muffin tin. Dust with some almond flour or ground almonds and tap off any excess flour to form a layer. Cut two strips of parchment paper and sit them into each compartment in a crisscross shape—this will help to remove the buns once they are ready.

For the crust, put the almond flour, coconut sugar and salt in the food processor and blitz to a fine flour consistency. Add the coconut oil and water and blend for a couple of minutes, until the mixture begins to form a dough consistency.

Distribute the mixture between the six muffin compartments and press the dough into the bottom and up the edges of each one. Leave a hollow center in the middle for the fillings!

To make the cherry jam, put the cherries, water and maple syrup in a saucepan and simmer for 10 to 15 minutes, until the cherries have softened and the mixture has reduced. Sift the cornstarch and add it to the saucepan, then cook for another 2 to 3 minutes while stirring constantly. Remove the saucepan from the heat and set aside to cool for 15 minutes.

Place 2 teaspoons (10 ml) of the jam in the center of each bun and set them aside in the fridge.

For the filling, put all of the frangipani ingredients in the food processor and blend to a paste. Spoon the mixture on top of the cherry filling, then even out the tops with a knife and place back in the fridge.

To make the icing, put the icing sugar, lemon juice, vanilla extract and almond milk in the food processor. Blend until smooth. Gradually add the coconut oil and pulse the mixture to incorporate, but do not overmix as the oil may split from the liquid.

Remove the buns from the muffin tin and sit them on a cooling rack. Spoon the icing on top of each bun, top with a cherry and serve.

Store in an airtight container in the fridge for up to 3 to 4 days.

Salted Caramel Donuts

Salt and caramel are one of those flavor combinations that I can never get tired of. These sweet and salty donuts are dense and full of flavor—perfect for taking with you on the go.

MAKES 6 TO 8 DONUTS

DONUTS

1 cup (100 g) rolled oats (use gluten-free if required)

½ cup (73 g) cashews

1 tbsp (9 g) maca powder

¼ tsp Himalayan pink salt

2 tbsp (30 ml) Salted Maca Caramel (page 155)

1 tbsp (15 ml) maple syrup

3 Medjool dates, pitted

GLAZE

2 tbsp (28 g) coconut oil (solid)

1 tbsp (15 ml) maple syrup

1 tbsp (15 g) cashew butter

½ tsp vanilla extract

⅛ tsp Himalayan pink salt

Flaked toasted almonds, for garnish

Coconut sugar, for garnish

Salted Maca Caramel (page 155, optional), for garnish

For the donuts, put the rolled oats, cashews, maca powder and salt in the food processor and blitz to form a floury consistency. Add the maca caramel, maple syrup and dates and blend until you have a sticky dough consistency.

Separate the dough into six to eight parts and roll them out into sausage shapes before placing them into a silicone donut mold. (If you don't have a mold, you can shape them into donuts with your hands.) Place them in the freezer to set for 30 minutes.

Meanwhile, prepare the glaze by heating the glaze ingredients in a double boiler over simmering water until they have melted. Whisk well until smooth and remove from the heat.

Line a tray or plate with parchment paper. Take the donuts out of the silicone mold and dip one side of them in the glaze. Put them on the prepared tray and freeze for 10 minutes to set.

Once set, remove the donuts from the freezer and dip them into the glaze for a second coating.

Sprinkle some flaked almonds and coconut sugar on top of the glaze and place them back in the freezer for another 5 minutes before serving. If desired, you can drizzle the donuts with some extra salted maca caramel.

These donuts can be stored in the fridge in an airtight container for up to 3 to 5 days.

Glazed Lemon and Poppyseed Donuts

Lemon and poppyseed are a classic flavor duo. The fresh lemon flavor means these donuts taste like a healthy lemon drizzle cake. These zesty no-bake donuts are much healthier than regular donuts, as they are free from any refined ingredients such as white flour or sugar.

MAKES 8 DONUTS

DONUTS

1 cup (100 g) rolled oats (use gluten-free if required)

½ cup (73 g) cashews

¼ tsp Himalayan pink salt

Zest of 1 organic lemon

2 tbsp (31 g) cashew butter

2½ tbsp (38 ml) maple syrup

1 tsp vanilla extract

1 tbsp (9 g) poppyseeds

GLAZE

2 tbsp (28 g) coconut oil (solid)

1 tbsp (15 g) cashew butter

1 tbsp (15 ml) maple syrup

1 tbsp (15 ml) lemon juice

Poppyseeds, for garnish

For the donuts, put the rolled oats, cashews and salt in a food processor and blitz until the ingredients reach a floury consistency. Add the lemon zest, cashew butter, maple syrup and vanilla extract and blend further until you have a dough consistency.

Transfer the dough to a large bowl and fold in the poppyseeds, then knead the dough to distribute them as evenly as possible.

Separate the dough into eight parts and roll them out into sausage shapes before placing them into a silicone donut mold. (If you don't have a mold, you can shape them into donuts with your hands.) Place them in the freezer for 30 minutes.

Meanwhile, prepare the glaze by heating the glaze ingredients in a double boiler over simmering water until the coconut oil has melted. Whisk until smooth and remove from the heat. Line a tray or plate with parchment paper. Take the donuts out of the silicone mold and dip one side of them in the glaze. Put them on the prepared tray and freeze for 10 minutes to set.

Once set, remove the donuts from the freezer and dip them into the glaze for a second coating.

Sprinkle some poppyseeds on top of the glaze and place them back in the freezer for another 5 minutes before serving.

These donuts can be stored in the fridge in an airtight container for up to 3 to 5 days.

Pumpkin Spice Latte Donuts

These are by far my favorite donuts. They even have a little coffee kick in the dough to live up to their name. If you love all things pumpkin spice, you have got to try these!

MAKES 6 TO 8 DONUTS

DONUTS

1 cup (100 g) rolled oats (use gluten-free if required)

½ cup (73 g) cashews

⅓ cup (63 g) coconut sugar

1 tsp pumpkin spice (see Note)

2 tbsp (20 g) instant coffee granules

¼ tsp Himalayan pink salt

1 tbsp (15 ml) pumpkin purée

4 Medjool dates, pitted

1 tsp vanilla extract

GLAZE

1½ tbsp (21 g) coconut oil (solid)

1 tbsp (15 ml) creamed coconut or coconut butter

1 tbsp (15 ml) maple syrup

½ tsp vanilla extract

Coconut sugar, for garnish

For the donuts, put the rolled oats, cashews, coconut sugar, pumpkin spice, coffee granules and salt in a food processor and blitz until the ingredients reach a floury consistency. Add the pumpkin purée, dates and vanilla extract and blend further until you have a dough consistency.

Separate the dough into six to eight parts and roll them out into sausage shapes before placing them into a silicone donut mold. (If you don't have a mold, you can shape them into donuts with your hands.) Place them in the freezer for 30 minutes.

Meanwhile, prepare the glaze by heating the glaze ingredients in a double boiler over simmering water until they have melted. Whisk well until smooth and remove from the heat.

Line a tray or plate with parchment paper. Take the donuts out of the silicone mold and dip one side of them in the glaze. Put them on the prepared tray and freeze for 10 minutes to set.

Once set, remove the donuts from the freezer and dip them into the glaze for a second coating. Sprinkle some coconut sugar on top of the glaze and place them back in the freezer for another 5 minutes before serving.

These donuts can be stored in the fridge in an airtight container for up to 3 to 5 days.

Note: If you can't find pumpkin spice, you can make your own by mixing 1 tablespoon (8 g) of ground cinnamon, 1 teaspoon of ground ginger, 1 teaspoon of ground nutmeg, ½ teaspoon of allspice and ½ teaspoon of ground cloves.

Decadent Chocolate

If you've ever wanted to make your own dairy-free chocolate from scratch, or simply haven't been able to find a store-bought version you've loved yet, this is for you.

Chocolate lovers, you've come to the right place. Over the past couple of years, I've been experimenting with different ingredients to make vegan-friendly chocolate. In this chapter, you'll find my perfected creamy Mylk Chocolate recipe (page 124), as well as a delicate white chocolate with real vanilla bean (page 128) and salted dark chocolate (page 127).

An important consideration when making delicious chocolate at home is that you need to avoid water getting into your chocolate mixture throughout the entire process. Chocolate recipes are based on fats, which don't like to mix with water. If liquid is added to the mix, it will cause the chocolate to seize, making your beautiful shiny chocolate dull and clumpy. Although you might be able to recover the mixture by adding more liquid, at this point it will be a ganache or a fudge and won't set like regular chocolate.

I find that cacao butter and cacao paste (otherwise known as cacao liquor) are best for making delicious vegan chocolate at home. The quality of the cacao you use will determine how good the end result of the chocolate will be, so be sure to buy pure cacao products that don't contain any added ingredients such as sugar or dairy.

To achieve professional-looking chocolate bars, I use silicone molds with the following measurements:

Dimensions: 8.35 x 4.1 x 0.4" (21.2 x 10.4 x 1 cm)
Cavity size: 6.3 x 3.1 x 0.4" (16 x 7.8 x 1 cm)
Volume: 3 oz (89 ml)

Mylk Chocolate with Cashews and Lucuma

Gluten-Free

The key to using coconut sugar but still avoiding a gritty texture in your chocolate is grinding down the coconut sugar to a powder in your food processor or blender. The finer the consistency of the sugar, the smoother the finished result of your chocolate. The addition of lucuma gives the chocolate a slight "caramel" flavor, while the addition of cashew butter makes it creamier than regular dark chocolate.

MAKES ABOUT 2 TO 3 LARGE BARS (9 OZ [255 G])

1 cup (218 g) raw cacao butter

⅓ cup (73 g) cacao liquor (cacao paste)

1½ tbsp (24 g) cashew butter

⅓ cup (63 g) coconut sugar

1 tbsp (8 g) lucuma powder

¼ tsp Himalayan pink salt

Put the cacao butter, cacao liquor and cashew butter in a medium-sized heatproof bowl, then place the bowl over a saucepan filled with simmering water to form a double boiler. Continue to heat gently over medium heat and stir until everything has melted evenly. Remove the bowl from the heat.

Put the coconut sugar, lucuma powder and salt in a blender or food processor and blend to a fine powder. The finer the powder, the smoother the end result of the chocolate. Sift the powder and add it to the bowl with the cacao mixture. Whisk well until smooth.

Pour the chocolate into silicone molds and allow it to cool for 5 minutes before carefully transferring the molds to the freezer to set for 1 hour.

After 1 hour, remove the chocolate from the molds and store in an airtight container in a cool place for up to 3 to 4 weeks.

Dark Chocolate with Maca and Sea Salt

Gluten-Free

The maca and coconut sugar together add a deep caramel flavor to the chocolate. Rounded off by sea salt, these sweet-and-salty treats are perfect for those who love their chocolate a little on the darker side.

MAKES ABOUT 2 LARGE BARS (7 OZ [198 G])

½ cup (109 g) raw cacao butter

½ cup (110 g) cacao liquor (cacao paste)

1 tbsp (14 g) coconut oil (solid)

1 tbsp (15 ml) creamed coconut or coconut butter (see Note)

⅓ cup (63 g) coconut sugar

1 tbsp (9 g) maca powder

¼ tsp sea salt

Put the cacao butter, cacao liquor, coconut oil and creamed coconut in a medium-sized heatproof bowl, then place the bowl over a saucepan filled with simmering water to form a double boiler. Continue to heat gently over medium heat and stir until everything has melted evenly. Remove the bowl from the heat.

Put the coconut sugar, maca powder and salt in a blender or food processor and blend to a fine powder. The finer the powder, the smoother the end result of the chocolate. Sift the powder and add it to the bowl with the chocolate mixture. Whisk well until smooth.

Pour the chocolate into silicone molds and allow the chocolate to cool for 5 minutes before carefully transferring the molds to the freezer to set for 1 hour.

Remove the chocolate from the molds and store in an airtight container in a cool place for up to 3 to 4 weeks.

Note: Creamed coconut (not to be mistaken with coconut cream) and coconut butter are essentially the same thing, made from the ground-up dried flesh of the coconut. It adds a great flavor to chocolate, works as a binding agent for bases and helps to set cheezecakes.

White Chocolate with Vanilla and Lucuma

Gluten-Free

I've tried several vegan white chocolate recipes and this is definitely the winner. The irresistible combination of white chocolate, delicate vanilla and sweet lucuma makes this recipe the perfect alternative to white chocolate made from dairy.

MAKES ABOUT 2 TO 3 LARGE BARS (10 OZ [283 G])

½ vanilla pod

1 cup (218 g) raw cacao butter

1 tbsp (15 ml) creamed coconut or coconut butter

1 tbsp (15 g) cashew butter

⅔ cup (79 g) icing sugar

1 tbsp (8 g) lucuma powder

¼ tsp Himalayan pink salt

Cut the vanilla pod in half and scrape out the seeds, put these in a medium-sized heatproof bowl along with the cacao butter, creamed coconut and cashew butter, then place the bowl over a saucepan filled with simmering water to form a double boiler. Continue to heat gently over medium heat and stir until everything has melted evenly. Remove the bowl from the heat.

Sift the icing sugar, lucuma powder and salt and add them to the bowl with the cacao butter. Whisk well until the mixture is smooth and without lumps.

Pour the chocolate into silicone molds and allow it to cool for 5 minutes before carefully transferring the molds to the freezer to set for 1 hour.

Remove the chocolate from the molds and store in an airtight container in a cool place for up to 3 to 4 weeks.

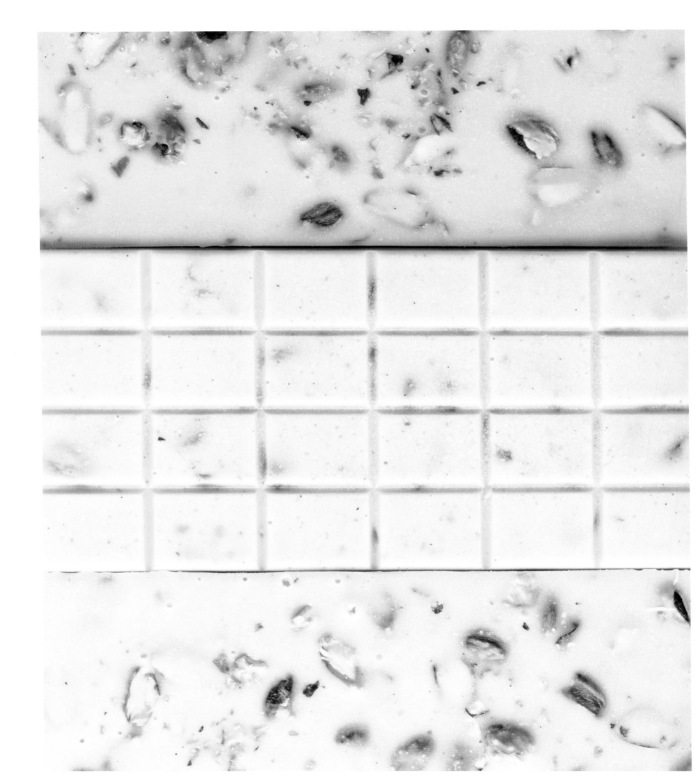

White Chocolate with Pistachios

When paired with the right ingredients, your cacao butter will transform into a delicious vegan version of white chocolate. This recipe combines white chocolate with fragrant pistachios for a luxurious flavor experience. The quality of cacao butter you use will determine the quality of your finished white chocolate. The cacao butter should smell like white chocolate when you open the packaging.

MAKES ABOUT 3 LARGE BARS (10.5 OZ [297 G])

1 cup (218 g) raw cacao butter (unmelted)

⅔ cup (79 g) icing sugar

½ tsp vanilla bean paste

2 tbsp (31 g) cashew butter

¼ tsp Himalayan pink salt

¼ cup (31 g) shelled pistachios

Put the cacao butter in a large bowl and heat in a double boiler over simmering water. Continue to heat gently over medium heat until all of the cacao butter has melted. Remove the bowl from the heat.

Sift the icing sugar and add it to the bowl with the cacao butter and whisk well. Then add in the vanilla bean paste, cashew butter and salt and continue to whisk until the mixture is smooth and without lumps.

Put some of the pistachios in the bottom of your silicone chocolate molds. Add the remaining pistachios to the white chocolate mixture and stir well to combine. Pour the chocolate into the molds and try to make sure the pistachios are distributed evenly.

Allow the chocolate to cool for 5 minutes before carefully transferring the molds to the freezer to set for 1 hour.

Remove the chocolate from the molds and store in an airtight container in a cool place for up to 3 to 4 weeks.

Gatherings and Special Occasions

Whether you're having a laid-back dinner party with friends or a more formal get-together with relatives or colleagues, these pastries and desserts pull out all the stops.

Growing up, I would always take the opportunity to create desserts for family occasions. At Christmas, I would usually make a selection of three or four dishes and took great pride in presenting them on large plates dusted with icing sugar. I remember how I found it difficult to pare back my ideas to just one flavor combination, hence there were always several elements to the desserts.

In the following pages, you'll find recipes that will be sure to impress your guests with remakes of classics like tiramisu (page 137), crème brûlée (page 141) and poached pears (page 134).

Creamy Poached Pears with Chamomile, Vanilla and Caramel

Gluten-Free

Fresh pears are slow-cooked in a creamy coconut milk sauce flavored with vanilla and chamomile before being slathered with sweet caramel sauce. This recipe works really well when paired with the Vanilla Bean and Chamomile Ice Cream recipe on page 78. The combination of warm and cold is a treat!

MAKES 4 SERVINGS

4 pears (Bosc and Concorde varieties work best)

1 vanilla pod

1 (13.5-oz [400-ml]) can full-fat coconut milk

2 tbsp (24 g) coconut sugar

6 chamomile tea bags

3 tbsp (48 g) homemade Salted Vanilla Bean–Cashew Butter (page 151) or store-bought cashew butter

3 tbsp (45 ml) maple syrup

Peel the skin from the pears, leaving the stalk intact.

Cut the vanilla pod in half and scrape out the seeds. Put both the seeds and the pod in a saucepan along with the coconut milk, coconut sugar and chamomile tea bags and heat over medium-low heat.

Whisk to combine all the ingredients and add the pears to the saucepan.

Cook the pears for approximately 1 hour over low heat, being careful not to boil the coconut milk, as it could separate. Turn the pears every so often to ensure that all sides cook evenly.

Once the pears are cooked "al dente," still firm in the middle, remove them from the heat. The coconut sauce will have reduced and thickened at this point.

Strain the remaining coconut milk sauce mixture through a fine-mesh sieve into a bowl to remove the tea bags and add the cashew butter and maple syrup. Whisk well to form a caramel sauce.

Plate the pears and drizzle with the caramel sauce. Serve immediately.

Layered Tiramisu
Gluten-Free

These layered jars are perfect for dinner parties. They can be prepared a day in advance and don't require any baking or long setting times. Each layer complements the next with the traditional tiramisu flavors of coffee, mascarpone, cacao and rum.

MAKES FOUR 10.2-OZ (289-G) JARS

CREAM TOPPING

1 (13.5-oz [400-ml]) can chilled coconut milk (using only the thick cream from the top of the can)

1 tbsp (15 ml) maple syrup

1 tsp vanilla extract

BASE

2 cups (234 g) walnuts

6 Medjool dates, pitted

⅛ tsp Himalayan pink salt

1 tbsp (10 g) instant coffee granules

1 tbsp (15 ml) boiling water

2 tbsp (30 ml) dark rum

MASCARPONE

1 vanilla pod

1¾ cups silken tofu (12.3-oz [350-g] block)

4 tbsp (60 ml) maple syrup

1 tbsp (15 ml) lemon juice

1 tbsp (14 g) coconut oil (solid)

½ cup (120 ml) chilled coconut milk (using only the thick cream from the top of a 13.5-oz [400-ml] can)

COFFEE SAUCE

2 tsp (7 g) instant coffee granules

1 tbsp (15 ml) boiling water

1 tbsp (15 ml) dark rum

2 tsp (4 g) cacao powder, plus more for garnish

2 tsp (10 g) almond butter

2 tsp (10 ml) maple syrup

For the cream topping, put the coconut milk, maple syrup and vanilla extract in a large bowl. Beat the mixture using an electric mixer until combined. Transfer the cream to a piping bag fitted with an open star tip, secure the top of the bag with an elastic band and refrigerate.

To make the base, put the walnuts, dates and salt in your food processor and blitz roughly. In a separate cup, mix together the coffee granules, boiling water and rum and add these to the food processor. Blend again until all the ingredients are combined. Set aside the base mix until you are ready to assemble the tiramisu.

For the mascarpone, cut the vanilla pod in half and scrape out the seeds using the back of a knife. Put the seeds in your high-speed blender along with the rest of the mascarpone ingredients and blend for a couple of minutes until smooth. Set aside.

To make the coffee sauce, simply put all the sauce ingredients in a small bowl and whisk until smooth.

To assemble, I used four 10.2-oz (289-g) jars, but you can use smaller jars if you want to make more portions.

Put a layer of the base in the bottom of each jar and top with a layer of the mascarpone. Follow this with 1 tablespoon (15 ml) of the coffee sauce. Repeat these layers so that you have two layers of each recipe component.

Pipe the cream topping on top of each serving jar and dust with cacao powder.

These desserts will keep in the fridge in an airtight container for up to 2 to 3 days.

Note: If you don't want to use alcohol in this dessert, replace the rum with half the amount of rum essence.

Salted Caramel and Vanilla Frozen Parfait Log

Gluten-Free

This frozen ice cream log is perfect for festivities or dinner parties. Adding maca powder to the caramel ice cream gives it a more intense caramel flavor. The caramel can be made with peanut butter for a rich peanuty taste or with cashew butter to be a more neutral caramel.

MAKES ONE 12-INCH (30.5-CM) LOG

VANILLA ICE CREAM LAYER

1½ cups (219 g) cashews (dry weight)

1 vanilla pod

1 (13.5-oz [400-ml]) can chilled coconut milk (using only the thick cream from the top of the can)

½ cup (120 ml) maple syrup

1 cup (240 ml) vanilla soy yogurt (use plain soy yogurt if preferred)

2 tbsp (28 g) coconut oil (solid)

CARAMEL ICE CREAM LAYER

1½ cups (219 g) cashews (dry weight)

1 (13.5-oz [400 ml]) can chilled coconut milk (using only the thick cream from the top of the can)

½ cup (120 ml) maple syrup

½ cup (120 ml) vanilla soy yogurt (use plain soy yogurt if preferred)

5 Medjool dates, pitted

2 tbsp (28 g) coconut oil (solid)

2 tbsp (18 g) maca powder

½ tsp Himalayan pink salt

SALTED CARAMEL SAUCE

2 tbsp (31 g) cashew butter (use peanut butter if preferred)

4 tbsp (60 ml) maple syrup

¼ tsp Himalayan pink salt

Coarse sea salt or Himalayan pink salt, for garnish

To prepare the cashews for the vanilla and caramel ice cream layers, soak the full 3 cups (438 g) in water for a minimum of 4 hours before rinsing with clean water and draining them, or quick soak in boiled water for 1 hour. Divide the soaked cashews into two parts for the separate vanilla and caramel ice cream layers.

For the vanilla ice cream layer, cut the vanilla pod straight down the middle and scrape out the seeds with the back of your knife. Put the vanilla seeds in a high-speed blender with the rest of the vanilla ice cream ingredients, including half of the soaked cashews. Blend until smooth and creamy. Line the bottom and sides of a 12-inch (30.5-cm) loaf pan with parchment paper. Pour the vanilla mixture into the pan and tap it gently on your work surface to knock out any air bubbles. Place in the freezer to set for at least 1 hour.

For the caramel ice cream layer, put all of the caramel ice cream ingredients, including the remaining half of the soaked cashews, in the high-speed blender and blitz until smooth. Get the pan out of the freezer, and gently pour the mixture on top of the vanilla layer and tap the pan on the counter again to knock out any air bubbles. Place in the freezer to set for 6 hours or overnight.

To prepare the salted caramel sauce, simply put all of the sauce ingredients in a bowl and whisk until smooth.

Once the parfait has set completely, remove it from the pan by turning it upside down and tapping gently. If it doesn't come out easily, you can wipe the outside of the pan with a hot, wet cloth.

Place the parfait on a serving platter and pour the sauce on top of it. Sprinkle with some coarse sea salt or Himalayan salt to garnish, then slice into serving portions.

Serve immediately, and place any leftovers straight back into the freezer in an airtight container.

Cardamom, Vanilla and Clementine Crème Brûlée

Gluten-Free

Crème brûlée is such an underrated dessert in my opinion. Not only is this version made dairy- and egg-free, I've jazzed it up with some exciting flavors of cardamom and clementine to give it a citrus twist. These brûlées are best served fresh. You can make them in advance and store them in the fridge; however, make sure you add the browned sugar topping just before serving.

MAKES 2 LARGE OR 3 SMALL BRÛLÉES

1 vanilla pod

1 (13.5-oz [400-ml]) can full-fat coconut milk

Zest of 2 clementines

10 cardamom pods (crushed)

⅓ cup (80 ml) maple syrup

2½ tbsp (20 g) cornstarch, sifted

Caster sugar, for garnish

Slice the vanilla pod down the center and scrape out the seeds. Put the seeds and the leftover pod in a saucepan with the coconut milk, clementine zest, cardamom pods and maple syrup. Gently warm over low heat for 5 minutes.

Pass the mixture through a fine-mesh sieve to remove the vanilla and cardamom pods. Put the liquid back in the saucepan.

Make a paste by putting the cornstarch in a bowl with 4 tablespoons (60 ml) of the coconut milk liquid. Mix well and add the paste to the saucepan. Bring the mixture to a simmer and whisk continuously for 5 minutes to cook out the cornstarch.

Pour the mixture into ramekins and allow to cool for 15 minutes before placing them in the fridge for at least 2 hours to set fully.

When you are ready to serve, add an even coating of caster sugar to the top of each dessert.

Finish each dessert using a blowtorch to give them a caramelized sugar coating.

Serve immediately.

Lemon and Lime Curd Tartlets

This recipe is a twist on classic lemon curd with the addition of zingy lime zest. They are made up of a lime-infused base and creamy lemon-lime filling. Optionally, you can top them with the soft meringue topping as seen in my Lemon Meringue Pie recipe on page 31.

MAKES FOUR 4-INCH (10.25-CM) TARTS

CRUST

2 cups (200 g) rolled oats (use gluten-free if required)

Grated zest of 1 organic lime

⅛ tsp Himalayan pink salt

5 Medjool dates, pitted

1 tbsp (14 g) coconut oil (solid)

1 tbsp (15 ml) lime juice

Additional coconut oil or olive oil, for greasing

Oat or almond flour, for dusting

LEMON-LIME CURD FILLING

1 cup (240 ml) chilled coconut milk (using only the thick cream from the top of a 13.5-oz [400-ml] can)

Grated zest of 2 organic lemons

Grated zest of 1 organic lime

Juice of 2 organic lemons

⅓ cup (80 ml) maple syrup

½ tsp agar-agar

1 tbsp (8 g) cornstarch

Soft Meringue Topping (page 32)

To make the crust, put the rolled oats, lime zest and salt in your food processor and blitz for a minute or so until you have a floury consistency. Add the dates, coconut oil and lime juice and blend until the mixture forms a dough consistency.

Grease the bottom of four tartlet tins with some coconut oil or olive oil and dust with the flour of your choice. Press the dough into the bottoms and sides of the tins and place in the fridge to rest while you prepare the filling.

For the filling, put the coconut milk, lemon zest, lime zest, lemon juice and maple syrup in a saucepan and bring to a simmer. Gently simmer over low heat for 5 minutes before passing the mixture through a fine-mesh sieve to remove the spent zest.

Separate ¼ cup (60 ml) of the liquid into a small bowl and whisk the agar-agar and cornstarch with it to form a paste. Place the remaining liquid back into the saucepan along with the paste and bring to a boil. Allow the mixture to cook for about 5 minutes while continuously whisking.

Once the mixture has thickened, remove it from the heat and allow to cool for 5 minutes before transferring it into the tartlet shells. Gently tap the tins on your work surface to knock out any air bubbles and allow to cool for 10 to 15 minutes before transferring the tartlets to the fridge to set for 4 hours.

Top the tartlets with soft meringue and use a blowtorch to brown the tops before serving.

These tartlets can be stored in the fridge in an airtight container for up to 2 to 3 days.

Note: Garnish with fresh lime wedges and lemon or lime zest if desired.

Blueberry-Vanilla Dessert Cubes

I like to use wild blueberries for this recipe, which give the dessert cubes a beautiful strong color and aromatic berry flavor. I love adding a hint of cinnamon to complement and intensify the berry taste. This dessert is as easy as blending each layer and allowing time for them to set.

MAKES 8 DESSERT CUBES

CRUST

½ cup (50 g) rolled oats (use gluten-free if required)

1 cup (146 g) cashews

¼ tsp ground cinnamon

¼ tsp Himalayan pink salt

4 Medjool dates, pitted

1 tbsp (14 g) coconut oil (solid)

BLUEBERRY LAYER

¾ cup (109 g) cashews (dry weight)

¼ cup (37 g) frozen blueberries, defrosted

¼ cup (60 ml) maple syrup

¼ cup (60 ml) chilled coconut milk (using only the thick cream from the top of a 13.5-oz [400-ml] can)

3 tbsp (45 ml) vanilla soy milk (or regular soy milk with ½ tsp vanilla extract)

1 tbsp (14 g) coconut oil (solid)

¼ tsp ground cinnamon

Ahead of time, prepare the total 1½ cups (219 g) cashews for both the blueberry and vanilla layers by soaking them in water for a minimum of 4 hours before rinsing with clean water and draining them, or quick soak in boiled water for 1 hour. Divide the soaked cashews into two parts for the separate blueberry and vanilla layers.

To make the crust, put the rolled oats, unsoaked cashews, cinnamon and salt in your food processor and blitz until they form a fine crumb consistency. Add the dates and blend further until they are broken down into the mixture. Lastly, add the coconut oil and blend again for a couple of minutes until everything has combined.

Press the dough into the bottoms of eight individual 2 x 2–inch (5 x 5–cm) cube-shaped silicone molds. (You can also use a baking dish or lunch box lined with parchment paper to make one large cake and cut it into cubes once it's frozen.)

Put all the ingredients for the blueberry layer, including half of the soaked cashews, in your high-speed blender and blitz until smooth and creamy without any lumps (the mixture should have a silky sheen to it).

Evenly distribute the mixture between the silicone molds and place them in the freezer to set for 1 hour. Make sure your blender is cleaned out for the next layer so that the blueberries don't stain the mixture.

VANILLA LAYER

¾ cup (109 g) cashews (dry weight)

¼ cup (60 ml) maple syrup

⅓ cup (80 ml) vanilla soy milk (or regular soy milk with 1 tsp vanilla extract)

1 tsp vanilla bean paste

2 tbsp (28 g) coconut oil (solid)

3 tbsp (45 ml) chilled coconut milk (using only the thick cream from the top of a 13.5-oz [400-ml] can)

1 tbsp (15 ml) lemon juice

¼ cup (37 g) frozen blueberries, defrosted

1 cup (148 g) fresh blueberries, for garnish

Fresh mint leaves (optional), for garnish

For the vanilla layer, put the remaining half of the soaked cashews, maple syrup, vanilla soy milk, vanilla bean paste, coconut oil, coconut milk and lemon juice in your high-speed blender and blitz until smooth without any lumps.

Transfer the mixture to a large bowl and gently fold the defrosted blueberries through the mix using a rubber spatula. Be careful not to overmix it—you want to create a marble effect with the berries.

Distribute the mixture evenly among the silicone molds and place them in the freezer to set for a minimum of 6 hours or overnight.

Once the dessert cubes are set, remove them from the silicone molds while still frozen.

Decorate the top of the desserts with fresh blueberries and mint, if desired. Defrost for 40 minutes to serve.

Store in the fridge in an airtight container for up to 2 to 3 days or freeze and defrost before serving.

See image on page 132.

Must-Haves

Complete your sweet vegan pantry with a stock of these delicious versatile spreads.

From dairy-free Notella (page 148) to vanilla bean–strawberry jam (page 152) and Salted Maca Caramel (page 155), these recipes make perfect additions to your no-bake desserts or toppings for your ice cream or breakfast oatmeal.

These dishes can be developed further and used as key elements in different recipes throughout the book. Try the Ferrawro Truffles on page 45 that are filled with my Notella recipe (page 148), or the Banoffee Cupcakes on page 113, which have a Salted Maca Caramel (page 155) surprise center.

Notella

Gluten-Free

I used to love this hazelnut-chocolate spread growing up. Unfortunately, the original version is full of dairy and sugar. My version is healthier and tastes just as great. Enjoy it on toast, as an addition to desserts, ice cream or oatmeal, or simply eat it straight from the jar!

MAKES ABOUT 10 OZ (283 G)

1 cup (135 g) skinless blanched hazelnuts

½ cup (120 ml) hazelnut milk

¼ cup (48 g) coconut sugar

2.5 oz (75 g) vegan-friendly chocolate (see page 124)

1 tbsp (14 g) coconut oil (solid)

¼ tsp Himalayan pink salt

½ tsp vanilla bean paste

To prepare the hazelnuts, heat a skillet over medium heat. Put the hazelnuts in the pan and toast them gently, tossing them every 30 seconds or so for about 5 minutes until they have browned slightly.

Transfer the hazelnuts to your food processor and pulse until they have blended down into a runny hazelnut butter. This can take anywhere from 5 to 15 minutes depending on the strength of your food processor. Make sure you scrape down the edges of the bowl every so often to make sure everything is blended evenly. Leave the hazelnut butter in the food processor for now, as you will be adding the rest of the ingredients to it.

In a saucepan, heat the hazelnut milk and coconut sugar over low to medium heat until all of the sugar has dissolved. Remove the pan from the heat and stir in the chocolate until it has melted.

Slowly add the chocolate mixture to the hazelnut butter over low-medium heat in the food processor and blend to incorporate. Add the coconut oil, salt and vanilla bean paste and blend to combine.

Transfer the Notella mixture to an airtight jar. For a silky, runnier consistency, store at room temperature and consume within a couple of days, otherwise you can store it in the fridge for a couple of weeks.

For extra creaminess, use an electric mixer to fluff up the mixture before serving.

Salted Vanilla Bean–Cashew Butter

Gluten-Free

I usually make all my nut butters at home from scratch, as it's much more cost effective. It's also tastier and you can get creative by adding different flavors like this salted vanilla bean–cashew butter. You can make this recipe in either a food processor or high-speed blender.

MAKES ABOUT 1¼ CUPS (313 G)

1½ cups (219 g) cashews

1 vanilla pod

1 tbsp (14 g) coconut oil (solid)

2 tsp (10 ml) maple syrup

¼ tsp sea salt

Put the cashews in a skillet over medium heat and toast to lightly brown them for about 5 minutes, tossing occasionally. Watch them carefully to make sure they don't burn.

Once the cashews have browned slightly, put them in the food processor and blend until they form a buttery consistency. This will take anywhere from 5 to 15 minutes, depending on the strength of your food processor. Scrape down the sides of the bowl every few minutes to ensure everything is mixed evenly.

Cut the vanilla pod in half and scrape out the seeds using the back of a knife. Add the vanilla seeds to the cashew butter along with the coconut oil, maple syrup and salt. Blend again for a couple of minutes until everything is mixed evenly.

Transfer the cashew butter to an airtight jar. Store at room temperature and consume within 1 week or keep it in the fridge for a few weeks.

Strawberry and Vanilla Bean Jam

Gluten-Free

One of my favorite jam combinations is this fragrant, sweet strawberry jam with a hint of warm, comforting vanilla bean. I love keeping a stash in the fridge and adding it to desserts, smoothies, porridge, plant-based yogurt or as a topping for homemade ice cream!

MAKES ONE 12-OZ (340-G) JAR

5¼ cups (782 g) frozen strawberries

½ cup (120 ml) water

Juice of ½ lemon

1 vanilla pod

¼ cup plus 1 tbsp (60 g) coconut sugar

2 tbsp (20 g) chia seeds

Put the strawberries, water and lemon juice in a saucepan and bring to a simmer over medium heat.

Meanwhile, slice the vanilla pod from top to bottom and scrape out the seeds. Add the seeds and vanilla pod to the saucepan along with the coconut sugar.

Stir well and bring the mixture to a boil. Once boiling, turn down the heat to medium and simmer for 30 to 40 minutes, until the mixture has reduced by about half.

Add the chia seeds to the saucepan and whisk well. Simmer for another 5 minutes and carefully remove the vanilla pod before setting the jam aside to cool.

Once cooled, transfer the jam to an airtight jar and store in the fridge for up to 1 week.

Salted Maca Caramel

Gluten-Free

This supereasy caramel is made with just a handful of ingredients in less than a few minutes. It doesn't require any special kitchen equipment and can be stored in the fridge and added to desserts, ice cream, porridge, nice cream, smoothies and more. Check out the Banoffee Cupcakes recipe on page 113 in which this is used as the filling.

MAKES ONE 10.2-OZ (289-G) JAR

½ cup (129 g) cashew butter
½ cup (120 ml) maple syrup
3 tbsp (27 g) maca powder
½ tsp Himalayan pink salt
1 tsp vanilla extract

Put all of the ingredients in a medium bowl. Whisk vigorously until you have a smooth paste without any lumps.

Transfer the caramel to an airtight jar and store in the fridge for up to 1 week.

Creamy Chocolate Whip

Gluten-Free

An ultra-creamy chocolate spread that is really simple to make. Just put your ingredients in a bowl and mix, no need for any special kitchen equipment. This chocolate whip is perfect with oatmeal, ice cream and desserts.

MAKES ABOUT 1 CUP (240 ML)

¼ cup (60 ml) vanilla soy yogurt (substitute with plain soy yogurt or coconut yogurt)

3 tbsp (47 g) cashew butter

3 tbsp (16 g) cacao powder, sifted

2 tbsp (30 ml) maple syrup

¼ tsp vanilla extract

Pinch of Himalayan pink salt

Put all of the ingredients in a medium bowl. Whisk vigorously until you have a smooth paste without any lumps.

Transfer the chocolate whip to an airtight jar and store in the fridge for up to 2 to 3 days.

Black Currant and Wild Blueberry Jam *Gluten-Free*

This jam is the perfect combination of tangy black currants and sweet blueberries. I love adding cinnamon to dark berries to enhance their flavor and add warmth. Try this jam with my Cinnamon-Blueberry Ice Cream (page 91), Vanilla Bean and Chamomile Ice Cream (page 78) or enjoy it with your porridge or on toast for breakfast.

MAKES ONE 10.2-OZ (289-G) JAR

1½ cups (150 g) frozen black currants

1 cup (155 g) frozen wild blueberries

¼ cup (60 ml) maple syrup

¼ tsp ground cinnamon

1 tsp vanilla extract

Put all of the ingredients in a saucepan and bring to a boil.

Turn down the heat to medium and simmer for 20 minutes, stirring often until most of the liquid has evaporated and the jam has thickened.

Once ready, remove the saucepan from the heat and set aside to cool.

Once cooled, transfer the jam to an airtight jar and store in the fridge for up to 2 weeks.

Acknowledgments

Creating this book has been an absolute dream come true for me, and it is the labor of many long days and nights spent writing, recipe testing, photographing and editing. It simply would not have been possible without the support and help from so many amazing people around me, to whom I am forever grateful.

Tom, thank you for always supporting me and putting up with me when I'm stressed. For your honesty with feedback on all of these recipes and for listening to me talk about this book for the past half year, I'm grateful to have you by my side.

To Sinead, for your words of encouragement throughout the many mornings, days and nights I spent writing this book. I am forever in debt to you for many more delicious treats and desserts, like it or not!

To my mom. My passion for creating most definitely stems from you. I have so many memories from when I was growing up of you making and creating, from playing piano by ear, to gardening and carpentry, to building homes for injured birds and setting them back into the wild. Thank you for raising us on your own, and working different jobs to make sure we never went without.

To my agent Nick and colleagues at No Logo Media who have been with me every step of the way. Thank you for working with me, guiding me, for your continued attention to detail, helping me realize my potential, and for making this book possible.

To my close circle of amazing friends and "dedicated taste testers." Your feedback on all of these recipes was so important to me in order to get them just right.

To the team at Page Street, for believing in me and giving me this exciting opportunity that a few years ago I could only have dreamed of. For your expertise and continuous work behind the scenes to help make this happen.

Kayla, thank you for all of your advice surrounding gluten-free ingredients, not to mention your constant love and support.

Ana, thank you for making space in your fridge and freezer and letting me borrow your beautiful kitchen!

Thanks to Matthew from MRN Photography for your amazing work with the author shots.

And to our community of followers and supporters at Addicted to Dates. Without you, this book would never have happened. Your support never goes unnoticed, and I greatly appreciate every comment, message, like, share, tag, recommendation and visit to the blog, as well as every one of you who tries out my recipes.

About the Author

Christina Leopold is the chef, author and self-taught photographer behind the recipe blog and Instagram account Addicted to Dates.

Christina obtained a degree in culinary arts; however, after working in a few kitchens during college placements, she decided that the food scene was not for her. She instead worked in sales, accounts and office management before pursuing a career as a full-time recipe developer and photographer.

Christina became vegan in 2015, and living between the rural areas in Cork and Kerry counties in Ireland meant vegan options were less readily available at the time, which led her back into the kitchen to start developing her own recipes.

Working long office hours from Monday to Friday, she would spend Friday nights creating in the kitchen and the rest of the weekend photographing and writing up recipes for her blog.

With a focus on wholesome, plant-based ingredients and minimally processed sugars, Addicted to Dates aims to help people re-create their favorite desserts in simple recipes, most of which don't even require an oven. Christina is passionate about showing and teaching people how to use plant-based ingredients as part of a vegan lifestyle.

Christina regularly gives cooking demonstrations at local Vegfests and also appeared at Vegan Life Live in London 2019. She loves travelling to give workshops and demonstrations.

When she's not creating in her kitchen, as a passionate animal rights activist, Christina spends her time volunteering for animal rights organizations and at vegan sanctuaries.

Christina's work has been featured by *Thrive* magazine, *Origin* magazine, *Vegan Food & Living*, feedfeed, Beautiful Cuisines, Best of Vegan and Vegan Bowls for Vegan Souls (the @coconutbowls cookbook). You can follow her on Instagram @addictedtodates.

Index